DISCOVERING THE STRUCTURE
OF SOCIAL STUDIES

Discovering
the
Structure
of
Social Studies

JAMES G. WOMACK

BENZIGER BROTHERS, NEW YORK

TO

my wife and parents

Acknowledgements

THE AUTHOR would like to express his gratitude and indebtedness to the many educators and scholars who offered encouragement and assistance in the preparation of this manuscript. Though it is not feasible to identify all by name, the author would like to extend a special word of appreciation to the following:

Dr. Gordon A. Wheaton, District Superintendent and Dr. Ernest F. Weinrich, Assistant District Superintendent, Board of Cooperative Educational Services, Third Supervisory District, Huntington, New York. Much of the pioneering work now taking place in the social studies in New York State can be traced to the enlightened leadership of Dr. Weinrich and the BOCES Cooperative Social Studies Project. The teacher-scholars who represent the six school districts participating in the BOCES Cooperative Social Studies Project are Barbara Brown, Norman Hollett, Paul King, Thomas Post, Mary Melia, Warren Moore, Margaret Norton, and Mildred Selby (Cold Spring Harbor School District), Margaret Baack (Elwood School District), Averam Silverman and Vincent Turner (Northport School District), Alan Gaynor (Smithtown School District), Eunice Crowley, Thomas Duffy, William Pratt, Clare Sharp, and Marjorie Wexler (South Huntington School District), Lavania Ferguson and Bert Gardner (Wyandanch School District).

The highly capable leadership that has been provided by Miss Mildred McChesney, Dr. Janet Gilbert, and others of the Bureau of Social Studies, New York State Education Department, Albany, New York has made New York State a leader in social studies curriculum reform. Much of the material in Chapter Six which relates to Understandings was taken directly from state publications, and has been used by the author not only in this book but in teacher training courses now being conducted in Suffolk County, Long Island.

The author would like to express his gratitude to Dr. Robert Johnstone, Chief of the Elementary Curriculum Bureau and Mr. Gordon Van Hooft, Chief of the Secondary Curriculum Bureau, New York State Education Department.

Foreword

THE CURRENT REVOLUTION in the *teaching* of social studies is represented by practically every educational agency in the country, including the Federal Government's Project Social Studies, the research divisions of the National Education Association, State Education Departments, numerous and widely separated universities and colleges, non-profit organizations, nationally prominent curriculum leaders, regional curriculum councils, and local curriculum committees.

The focus of social studies curriculum groups has changed imperceptibly from grade allocation of content to the instructional methods used by teachers. This does not mean, of course, that curriculum research is not continuing to foster changes in social studies content. All of us are well aware that more substantive material is being forced down into the primary grades; that the amount of material to be covered and the repetition of coverage are being reduced; that more in-depth case study materials are being used; that more attention is being given to the study of non-Western cultures; and that schools are offering an ever-increasing number and variety of social studies electives to their seniors. These content trends are important, but they have been totally eclipsed by the changes which are being so forcefully proposed for teaching methodology.

One scholar after another in recent years has set down the major principles of the social sciences and attested to the great value they could have for social studies instruction. These prominent scholars, who include Professors Senesch of Purdue, Hanna of Stanford, and Bruner of Harvard, have been joined by other scholars associated with Educational Services Incorporated, the National Education Association, the Educational Research Council of Greater Cleveland, the state education departments of New York and California, and numerous universities including Stanford, Syracuse, and Wisconsin.

These esteemed individuals and organizations have given considerable merit to the thesis that the aims of instruction in the social studies should be the students' discovery of the principles and generalizations of the field, rather than the traditional coverage and mastery of unrelated content. The remainder of this publication expands on this thesis and proposes a practical approach for its implementation.

This publication sets forth the nature of this methodology revolution, details its requirements, advantages, and implications for the classroom teacher, and offers practical suggestions, including model units, to assist the teacher in preparing his own units and employing this new methodology in his classroom.

Introduction

IN THE PAST FIVE YEARS, one curriculum group after another has called for a teaching methodology which will include an interdisciplinary approach to social studies content or will use social studies principles and generalizations as the major anticipated outcomes of learning. Recently, some groups have been urging combining the two into an *interdisciplinary approach to generalizations in the social studies.*

The calls for an interdisciplinary approach to generalizations have met a warm reception from the informed social studies teacher. For him it holds the promise of reawakening his own interest in his chosen field, helping him select and organize course content, assisting him in having students discover for themselves the underlying structure of the social sciences, and most importantly serving him and the students as worthwhile goals for social studies instruction.

This publication outlines in detail how these and other worthwhile goals can be successfully met by the teacher who is competent in using the interdisciplinary approach to generalizations.

The first five chapters deal exclusively with generalizations. Chapter One describes the four types of generalizations, while Chapter Two concentrates on the most important type, substantive generalizations. Chapters Three and Four point out the functions and limitations of generalizations, respectively, while Chapter Five concludes Section I by illustrating some typical test items for evaluating students' understanding of generalizations.

Chapter Six identifies and characterizes social studies concepts and understandings. The process of concept formation is outlined with suggested test items for concepts identified. Included is a description of the interrelationship of generalizations and concepts, and a chart suggesting how the teacher's planbook might be organized to show this relationship. The chapter ends with a consideration of social studies understandings, their relationship to generalizations, and some dangers of over-extending this relationhip.

Chapter Seven focuses on the interdisciplinary approach and the need for using all social science disciplines in gaining a comprehensive understanding of the content. The uniqueness of each discipline is exemplified by economics, while the skills and techniques of the social science are given the lion's share of attention.

Chapter Eight ties all the important points raised in the previous chapters into a composite methodology with each part identified, described, and analyzed. A model unit on U. S. immigration policies further illuminates the intricacies of the methodology. Eight other model units have been added in the appendix to further illustrate the interdisciplinary approach to generalizations.

Chapter Nine, A Plan of Action for Developing A K-12 Social Studies Program, details the exact sequence of steps that curriculum leaders and teachers in a local school system should take to develop a K-12 social studies curriculum focusing on an interdisciplinary approach to generalizations.

... the curriculum of a subject should be determined by the most fundamental understanding that can be achieved of the underlying principles that give structure to that subject.

JEROME BRUNER
Process of Education, p. 31.

Contents

DISCOVERING THE STRUCTURE
OF SOCIAL STUDIES

CHAPTER 1

Four Types of Social Studies Generalizations

WHEN A PRINCIPAL enters the classroom of the mathematics teacher, he finds the students concentrating on a principle or theorem of the particular course or he sees them developing a specific mathematical skill, such as factoring, substituting, changing signs, or plotting coordinates. When he enters the social studies classroom, he finds the students being exposed to facts, details, and content. Rarely does he expect to find a principle or generalization being evolved or a particular skill being introduced or refined, and rarely is he disappointed in his expectation. This is not to indict the teachers of social studies or to challenge their effectiveness. What they are doing in the classroom, they are doing rather well. It is what they are not doing but should be doing which merits and receives attention here.

That the social sciences have basic principles or rules is an incontrovertible fact. That these principles can meet all the rigorous standards expected from mathematical principles is seriously doubted. Certainly, they can not be tested in the same scientific manner. Nevertheless, one scholar after another in recent years has set down the major principles of the social sciences and attested to the great value they could have for social studies instruction.

The Definition and Characteristics of Generalizations

A generalization is a broad inclusive statement in complete grammatical sentence form which serves as a principle or rule for the social studies. Its characteristics include the following:

1. Generalizations are derived from social studies content, but they are not content themselves. They not only have content as their source, but their substantiation and proof for being generalizations also come from content.

2. Generalizations have universal application and admit no major exceptions.

3. Generalizations contain no specific references to any particular peoples, places, or times.

4. Generalizations have a thesis; that is, they make a point about the subject of the sentence.

5. Generalizations, as principles or rules, comprise the underlying structure for each social science discipline.

6. Generalizations are best discovered by inductive reasoning.

7. Generalizations are abstractions which can be broken down into gradations of complexity and completeness so that they can be understood and mastered, to some extent, even by primary grade students.

8. Definitions and concepts are not themselves generalizations, but may be incorporated into a generalization.

These qualities of generalization can best be understood by offering two examples each from the social science diciplines.

Examples of Generalizations from Geography

1. The particular movements of rotation and revolution of the earth in space cause variations among its geographic regions, and these variations in turn affect how man lives in different regions of the earth.

2. Natural resources are insignificant if unused by man, and if used, their manner of use reflects man's wants as well as his level of technology.

Generalizations from Economics

1. Since natural resources are limited and human wants unlimited, every society has developed a method for allocating its scarce resources.

2. A division of labor takes advantage of the special competencies of each member of the work force, thereby leading to increased productivity.

Generalizations from Political Science

1. Every society has had rules, written or unwritten, by which social control over the people's conduct is maintained.

2. As the powers of government are concentrated in the hands of a few, the possibility of dictatorship increases and the possibility of democracy decreases.

Generalizations from History

1. The constants of history are change and continuity, and for each the goal is progress as that society sees progress.

2. Though the events of history give the appearance of repetitiveness, each event has certain qualities which make it unique.

Generalizations from Anthropology

1. Homo sapiens are of one single species, and though differences exist among groups of humans, the differences are not necessarily inequalities.

2. A person's culture, its mores and traditions, affects his thinking, perceiving and feeling throughout life.

Generalizations from Sociology

1. In all societies, the functions of socialization and acculturation are tasks of the family, and every society has developed rather complex, lengthy processes by which it prepares its youth for induction into society.

2. In general, the more mature the society, the greater its reliance on formal institutions for maintaining social control.

Generalizations from Social Psychology

1. Man's development of human traits and his perception of himself as a particular personality derive from his group associations.

2. Behavior is a result rather than a cause, and usually reflects the particular social needs of the individual.

The aforementioned generalizations deal with content and are called substantive generalizations and though they are our primary concern, there are three other types of generalizations which merit consideration.

Sub-Generalizations

A second type of generalization, the sub-generalization, differs from the substantive generalization in that it has limited rather than universal application. The degree of application is usually identified by an introductory phrase of the sentence. Some examples of sub-generalizations follow:

1. *In a capitalist country,* the regulator of supply and demand is the market place.

2. *In fascist countries,* the people are the servants of the state rather than served by the state.

3. *In the Common Market countries,* the principle of regional specialization has led to increased trade with mutual benefit for all.

Sub-generalizations have less value for our purposes, but the teacher should be aware of them in order to prevent students' confusing them with the substantive generalizations which have unlimited application.

Methodological Generalizations

A methodological generalization is a principle or rule which describes a skill or technique for studying social studies content.

Some examples of methodological generalizations are:

1. Areal geographic relations can be seen most readily by the use of map symbols and scales.

2. Prior to attempting any measurement, as with gross national product or the number of eligible voters, it is important to establish a precise definition of each term to be measured.

3. Inductive thinking in the social sciences has the asset of predictability and the debit of uncertainty, since its focus is on establishing a pattern for a finite number of observable phenomena.

4. Any adequate comparison of political systems demands the establishment of multiple criteria.

5. Few events have single causes or single results.

6. In any system of classification, such as polling, sampling, or establishing categories, one must first establish limits and characteristics for the elements to be included in the classification system.

These methodological generalizations are very important in the interdisciplinary approach to generalizations and are to be taught as an integral part of skill development and should not be left to chance. Their place of importance is made clearer in Chapter Seven where the focus is on an interdisciplinary approach rather than on the discovery of generalizations.

A fourth type of generalization, and the one most open to challenge as a true generalization, is the normative generalization. These generalizations express a value judgment and thus often take the form of sub-generalizations with only limited application. Examples of normative generalizations are:

1. In the democratic system of government, the individual is served by the state and is the master of the state; however, this relationship is reversed in fascist or communistic systems of government.

2. Democracy has survived only because of the role played by political parties.

3. Competition promotes excellence that would never appear in a more cooperative atmosphere.

4. Throughout history, man's incentive to advance has been his desire to attain material wealth rather than to serve the cause of humanity.

The normative generalizations do not have the credibility, universal application, or the objectivity of our substantive generalization, and for most purposes, the teacher needs to be aware of them only to avoid their use in the classroom.

It is indisputable that normative generalizations carry a certain degree of indoctrination since they are value judgments. Teachers must be alert to the danger that students may convert the thesis of a sub-generalization, having limited application, into a normative generalization with universal application. Thus, the sub-generalization, "The market place is the most efficient regulator of supply and demand *in capitalist countries,*" must not be converted into the normative generalization, "The market place is the most efficient regulator of supply and demand."

SUMMARY

Of the four types of generalizations—substantive, methodological, sub-generalization, and normative—two do not meet our full criteria for generalizations.

They are the sub-generalization and the normative generalization. The degree to which the teacher will find either of the two valuable will vary with the refinement the teacher requires of the students in their usage. Certainly, the teacher must not allow them to pass for substantive generalizations. If students use them, the teacher must consistently stress their limited application and their judgmental, subjective nature.

For our purpose, the emphasis is on substantive generalizations, and to a lesser extent, methodological generalizations.

CHAPTER 2

Substantive
Generalizations

SUBSTANTIVE GENERALIZATIONS are rules or principles expressed in complete sentence form which have universal application and which may be inductively reasoned from the contents of the social studies. In their most refined state, generalizations are abstractions.

Since generalizations are abstractions, they have the important quality of being able to be gradated in complexity and completeness so that students of any grade level can, to some meaningful extent, master their significance. Thus, any generalization can be formulated and worded so that it retains its essence and thesis, while its complexity and completeness can be made appropriately abstract for a primary or high school student. This simply means that generalizations, like all abstractions, have degrees of complexity and completeness and thus can be formulated into an appropriate degree of abstraction for any student without loss of the essence of the principle.

This quality of gradations of abstraction enables generalizations to serve as a major articulating strand for the entire K–12 social studies curriculum. An example will clarify this articulating function of generalizations.

In the primary grades, the students could master a generalization having a degree of abstraction such as:

7

All families divide the work among the family members so they can meet their basic needs.

For the intermediate grade student, the appropriate degree of abstraction for the same generalization might be:

A division of labor takes advantage of the best skills of each member of the family or any working group.

For the junior high student, the same generalization might increase in abstraction to read:

A division of labor produces specialized workers, thereby leading to an increase in the production and quality of goods.

And finally, for a senior high student, the same generalization could be made rather sophisticated and abstract, so that it might read:

A division of labor leads to increased productivity and a rising standard of living.

The appropriate degree of abstraction of generalizations for students at any particular grade or ability level is, of course, a decision to be made by the teacher. It seems very likely that in the near future, the teacher will have available an authoritative list of generalizations in their most abstract form.

The Stanford Social Studies Project under Dr. Paul Hanna has already produced an unrefined list of more than 3500 generalizations. This list, though tentative and needing synthesis, can be used now by any teacher as a guide to select the generalizations pertinent to the content of his course. A teacher, after extracting from this list of 3500 generalizations those which he feels students might discover from the content of the course, would then reduce the abstraction of the selected generalizations until they were appropriately complex and complete for the particular grade and ability level of his students.

If the activity outlined in the foregoing was done cooperatively by social studies teachers representing all grades from kindergarten to twelve, Table 2.1 would be a valuable guide.

<small>TABLE 2.1.</small>

Generalizations for a K–12 Social Studies Curriculum

Priority generalizations which all students should master in their most abstract form	Grade levels where each generalization would be taught	Degree of abstraction appropriate to each of these grade levels
The supply and demand of particular categories of workers leads to wage and standard of living differentials and thereby stratification of social classes	3—5—7—9—12	**Grade 3.** Some workers make more money than others because their services are needed more. **Grade 5.** Both the supply of workers and the demand for workers operate to determine the wages paid for particular kinds of workers. **Grade 7.** The more income one has the greater his claim on the goods available, and thus the higher his standard of living. **Grade 9.** The standard of living a person has is a major criteria for determining the social class to which he belongs. **Grade 12.** The supply and demand of particular categories of workers leads to wage and standard of living differentials, and thereby stratification of social classes.

A completed table such as Table 2.1 would provide a school system with a social studies curriculum articulated by one of the aims of instruction, namely generalizations.

The Use of Inductive Thinking to Discover Generalizations

Generalizations are not an integral part of social studies content. That is, one does not open any social studies text and find generalizations written out. However, they are there and can be discovered by a process of inductive thinking.

Inductive thinking may be defined as a mental skill wherein an observer sees a finite number of items, parts, events, or phenomena and reasons that each of them falls into a particular pattern based on some criteria such as size, shape, quantity, order, or distance. Since they do fit into a certain pattern, the observer can make a cautious prediction concerning the next phenomena, its size, shape, quantity, order, or distance. Inductive thinking has that marvelous scientific asset of predictability, but it also has the defect of uncertainty, since the validity of the prediction rests solely on the perceived pattern of events holding true to form.

Two examples help to illustrate the previous points.

Let us say our observer sees a group of numbers in a series such as:

$$3 \qquad 8 \qquad 18 \qquad 33 \qquad 53.$$

Is he in a position to inductively perceive a pattern among the members of the series, and if so, can he predict the next higher number? Yes, most certainly the observer could perceive that each number of the series is separated from the previous number by multiples of five, beginning with one 5. Thus five digits separate 3 from 8, ten digits separate 8 from 18, and so on. If a teacher is able to inductively reason that this pattern of multiples of 5 separates the numbers of the series, then he can predict that the next number following 53 would be 78.

A second example of inductive thinking will further amplify the inductive process of thinking. In studying analogies, and parenthetically the social sciences are replete with analogies, the colon sign : is read "is to." Thus the expression A:B is read A is to B; the expression B:C, is read B is to C. Thus an analogy such as A:B (as) B:C is read "A is to B (as) B is to C." That is, they are related in some similar way, whether it be size, shape, quantity, distance, or whatever. Inductive thinking permits the observer to answer such analogies as:

raw: war (as)_____: wolf
or
not: _____ (as) era: are

In both examples the pattern is that the order of the letters of the words is reversed. The respective answers are *flow* and *ton*.

Students, with guidance from teachers, must use inductive thinking if they are to discover social studies generalizations from a body of content. The process of inductive thinking must be developed over long periods of time before it becomes sophisticated; however, it can be taught to students to some operational extent in only a few class periods. Sophistication comes with experience, and the search for generalizations not only offers this experience, but serves as the aim of the experience.

Before students can begin to think inductively about any generalizations which may be imbedded in a body of content, the teacher must arrange the learning activities of the unit so that students are exposed to all or most of the factual strands, which, when organized into a pattern, will constitute a generalization. This is to assert that the teacher can not reasonably expect his students to arrive at a particular generalization—which the teacher has in mind from the very beginning of the unit— unless the learning activities, classroom discussions, lectures, reading and writing assignments, audiovisual materials, and class activities are arranged in a manner whereby the factual content presented contains the many strands of the generalization.

Thus, in a 9th grade unit of study on modern China, the teacher may have a particular sociological generalization, among several generalizations, he feels the students should be able to inductively reason from the content of the unit. However, before the students can begin to reason toward this generalization, the teacher knows that they must be exposed to the factual content containing the strands of the generalization. Let us say the sociological generalization is imbedded in the content surrounding the internal events which took place in China following the Japanese invasion of 1937.

The teacher realizes that his students must know this particular content if he expects them to eventually arrive at the sociological generalization. He arranges his teaching methods and materials to make sure they are exposed to the content. He examines the students to determine if they have a fair grasp of the content. He may ask them to put the facts in summary form such as the following:

Prior to the Japanese invasion of North China in 1937, China was torn apart by internal squabbles between various factions of the Kuomintang and the Communists. However, when the powerful Japanese ground forces threatened to subjugate the whole of China, the internal groups joined together and formed a tenuous united front. This united front, though often strained, managed to hold China together and with allied aid saw the war end with Japan defeated and removed from the Chinese mainland. Once the Japanese had been eliminated as a serious threat, the united front collapsed and the internal chaos reappeared.

The next step is to ask the students to outline the pattern of events which took place in China, omitting any reference to China, Japan, or any period of time. The students would quickly submit that the events followed a pattern such as: (1) factions within a country were fighting each other; (2) an external force appeared which both factions recognized as a threat to the whole country and to each of them; (3) the internal factions pooled their efforts to combat this common enemy; and (4) with the defeat of the enemy, the joint effort collapsed and the internal struggle reappeared.

Once agreement is reached on this as the pattern of events, the teacher can ask the students to inductively reason, in one complete sentence, a generalization by combining the strands of the pattern of events. The class should arrive at a generalization such as:

Internally warring factions will join together when each perceives an external force as mutually threatening and will tend to separate when the external force is no longer perceived as threatening.

or

Internal dissension will be reduced when an external force is viewed as a threat to all and will tend to reappear when the threat no longer exists.

Please notice that in using the words, *internally warring factions*, the generalization immediately becomes applicable to many groups, such as labor unions, students, armies, democracies, and so on.

In summary of these points the teacher should follow a sequential order of procedure.

First   Decide on the generalization(s) the students should discover from a particular unit of study.

Second   Organize the learning activities and materials in a manner which exposes the strands or parts of the generalization(s) to the students.

Third   Ask the students to write a summary of the content which contains the generalization(s).

Fourth   Ask the students to identify the sequence of the pattern of events comprising the content, omitting any references to any particular peoples, places, or times.

Fifth   Ask the students to synthesize the various parts of the pattern of events into one complete sentence which purports to be a generalization.

Sixth   Ask the students to offer proof that their statement is, in fact, a generalization by citing examples that it existed and operated in other periods, places, and among other people. This citation of proof stage will be further explained in Chapter 8.

This is only one of several possible ways in which students may be helped to think inductively in their search for generalizations.

Like most mental processes, the person's efficiency increases with experience.

Deductive Thinking and Using Generalizations

We have limited ourselves thus far to the role of inductive thinking in discovering generalizations. Deductive thinking also has a role involving generalizations. From the outset, it should be made clear that inductive thinking helps primarily in *discovering* generalizations, while deductive thinking helps in *applying* the generalization to another situation or body of content.

Deductive thinking is more difficult in the social sciences than in mathematics for the reason that in mathematics the subject under discussion can usually be put into an "all" category, whereas this is rarely the case with factual social science content. Thus, in mathematics, we are acquainted with innumerable examples of deductive syllogisms such as:

> *All* A is less than one-half the size of *all* B.
> *All* B is more than twice the size of *all* C.
> Thus *All* B is more than the sum of *all* A and C.

Mathematically expressed, it would look like the following:

$$A < \tfrac{1}{2}B$$
$$B > 2C$$
$$B > A + C$$

In social studies, we are very limited in the number of factual events or items we could put into an "all" category. To compound the problem, we would fall into the argument over the precise meanings of our social studies terms. An example points out the weaknesses of using deductive syllogisms in social studies.

All Anti-Federalists opposed the Constitution's elastic clause.

> T. Jefferson was an Anti-Federalist.
> T. Jefferson opposed the elastic clause.

In this syllogism, the conclusion is true but the premise is false; not *all* Anti-Federalists opposed the elastic clause.

Thus, we are on shallow ground if we put an "all" premise to factual deductive syllogisms concerning social studies content. We can use deductive thinking, however, in applying generalizations to other content. Deductive thinking can add significance and predictability to a pattern of events when that pattern of events is similar to another pattern the students have already studied and from which they have derived generalizations. For example, the generalization, *Internally warring forces will join together when they perceive an external force as threatening and will tend to separate when the external force is removed*, adds meaning and predictability to social studies topics such as:

1. the reaction of the American people following the bombing of Pearl Harbor;

2. the reaction of the British during the Luftwaffe night raids;

3. the reaction of a family when threatened by an external force;

4. the reaction of most social institutions when mutually threatened by an external force; as the reaction of labor unions to the Taft-Hartley Law.

A second example which shows how a generalization, once mastered, can be used to facilitate learning other content is *As the powers of governments are concentrated in the hands of a few people, the possibility of dictatorship increases while the possibility of democracy decreases.* The students' mastery of this generalization permits them to gain additional significance and some historical predictability from a subsequent study of content such as:

1. the process of Adolf Hitler becoming the German Chancellor, usurping the powers of the office of President of Germany, gaining control over Germany's military forces, and eventually becoming the dictator of Germany;

2. the process of Stalin gaining the powers of Secretary of the Communist party, and Premier of the U.S.S.R., and becoming

the leading member of the Politburo and the Communist Party Central Committee;

3. the reasons for the separation of powers in our Federal constitution;

4. the reason why most governments, businesses, and social institutions prevent multiple office-holding by a single individual.

SUMMARY

Inductive thinking can be used by students to discover for themselves the generalizations of the social studies. Deductive thinking, though having less value as a discovery tool, has significant worth in applying a known generalization to other content. For the child who progresses up the K–12 social studies curriculum, it is expected that his training prior to junior high school would consist primarily of inductive thinking to discover generalizations. From the junior high grades through public schooling and adult life, the individual would employ both inductive and deductive thinking when confronted with new thoughts imbedded in new content.

CHAPTER 3

The Functions of Generalizations

GENERALIZATIONS can serve four important functions in a K–12 social studies curriculum. Briefly listed they are:

1. as a major aim of social studies instruction;
2. as a major guide to select the social studies content for each grade level;
3. as a major criterion for organizing and arranging the content and learning activities for each unit of study;
4. as a major principle for articulating the entire K–12 curriculum for social studies.

Using Generalizations as a Major Aim of Social Studies

The aims of social studies are listed in hundreds of sources. They invariably include developing good citizenship traits, mastering a specified amount and kind of content, being able to use certain social studies skills, and developing some understanding of the nature of the social science disciplines, particularly history and geography. This author has no objection to any of these worthwhile aims of social studies, recognizing in most every instance, however, that they lack specificity. Serious objections can be leveled, however, at any statement of aims in any field of study when the underlying principles and generalizations of the discipline have been omitted from the statement.

Certainly, if the mastery of the factual content of a discipline merits consideration as an aim of instruction, then undoubtedly the principles and generalizations which relate the facts, one to another, and gives them meaning and applicability to new situations, can hardly be excluded as a major aim of instruction.

Now that research groups are making available their findings on generalizations, the probability of including generalizations as instructional aims is very strong. Any state education department or school district can take a giant step forward by compiling an authoritative list of generalizations for each course in the K–12 social studies curriculum. Such a giant step would not be too difficult since a synthesis of available lists would satisfy most immediate needs. The bibliography on page 136 serves as a beginning for such a list of generalizations.

Using Generalizations to Help Select Content

Probably the most irrefutable and damaging criticism of social studies is the ever-increasing amount of content the teacher is expected to cover and the students are supposed to learn. The result of this practice has been "covering ground" so that the state syllabus requirements are met.

In recent years, an irrepressible trend has developed among state education departments and curriculum leaders to select for study only that content which *must* be mastered, and to leave any omitted content to the discretion of the teacher as to its merit for his students. The ground rules for selecting even the content which *must* be studied are hazy and haphazardly applied.

It seems incontestable that the aims of instruction, our generalizations for instance, should be a major guide for selecting content. The rule to follow in selecting content should be: the content which best lends itself to the students' discovery of priority generalizations will be selected for study. To put it differently, once it is agreed that the aim of social studies instruction should be the discovery of generalizations, then that content of each prescribed course is selected which best lends itself to this aim.

With an authoritative list of generalizations on hand, it would be a simple matter to select the content for the course. If the teacher, for example, taught the traditional fifth grade course in American history, he would immediately have some indication as to the types of generalizations to select from the authoritative list. He would select only those generalizations from history and geography, and any other social sciences, which are contained in the general nature of the content of the course.

He would then choose those particular generalizations which any fifth grade student should master. The next step would be to determine the generalization which could best be discovered from certain parts of the course content, and then decide on a priority listing of the generalizations.

This approach of using generalizations to select content will not solve all the problems caused by the inexorable flow of content into the social sciences. But, it would be very valuable to decide on the content which could be omitted simply because the content had very little significance for the aim of the course, namely, generalizations.

To recapitulate, the steps in this procedure of using generalizations to select content are:

1. Compile an authoritative list of generalizations.

2. Choose from the list those generalizations which most likely can be discovered from the prescribed content of the course.

3. Arrange the chosen generalizations in a priority order of those which must be learned to those which may or may not be necessary for the particular course.

4. Decide which of the *must* generalizations the students can discover from a particular unit of study. The teacher now has a list of generalizations that students can discover unit by unit.

5. Decide which unit has generalizations that absolutely must be learned and which has generalizations that could be omitted if necessary.

6. Arrange the units with the *absolutely must* generalizations in a sequence based on one of the usual criteria, such as chronology, expanding environments, or topical approach.

Since generalizations will rarely be the sole aim of social studies instruction, they would have to be considered along with any other aims or goals before any content is omitted.

Using Generalizations to Organize the Learning Activities

If generalizations are to serve as the aim of the unit of study and are to be inductively reasoned from a body of content, then it is imperative that the teacher arrange the learning activities of the class in a manner which will ensure that the students are fully exposed to the particular content of the unit containing the generalizations. The students are most likely to discover a generalization from content when they have been exposed to that content in a variety of manners. These include the commonly accepted instructional methods of lecture, discussion, text and outside reading assignments, and audio-visual presentations. The point being that students are most likely to perceive generalizations from content, when they have been exposed to the content in all its myriad forms. The learning activities must be organized and arranged in a manner so that each activity permits the students to see a new strand or part of a generalization.

Using Generalizations for Articulation

Generalizations have as one of their major functions the articulating of the K–12 social studies curriculum. Vertical articulation may be defined as the organizing of the courses in a field of study, such as social studies, in some orderly sequence based on a definite criteria. The criteria may be one of chronology, expanding environments, functions of man, or a topical approach.

It is a common practice to have more than one criterion articulating the K–12 social studies curriculum. Most frequently the lower grades, K-4, are articulated by an "expanding environment" thread, while the grades of 5-12 are articulated by chronology. It is also quite common to find that the aims of the field of study are rarely able to be adapted as articulating principles. Such is not the case with generalizations.

Since generalizations are abstractions rather than an integral part of the social studies content, they can be easily formulated into varying degrees of abstraction so that their complexity and completeness is appropriate for any grade level. Thus, the same generalization, varying in degrees of abstraction, can be meaningfully mastered by a primary student as well as the high school senior. This marvelous trait permits generalizations to serve as the overall framework to hold together the changing content of the social studies as students move from one grade to the next.

In the course of following the K–12 curriculum in social studies, the child may discover the same generalization in a variety of content, the only difference being the teacher's insistence that the student formulate the generalization to a degree of abstraction which is appropriate for that particular grade level. Such a continuing experience of discovering and formulating generalizations over a K-12 curriculum would permit a student to gain unusual proficiency in this skill, and to develop the habit of using it throughout adult life.

As a major articulating principle for the K–12 social studies curriculum, generalizations have several advantages over most of the commonly used articulating principles. First, generalizations can articulate the entire K–12 curriculum and not just segments of it. Second, it is one of the few aims of instruction which can also serve as an articulating principle. Third, generalizations can be used concurrently with other articulating principles, without mitigating the effectiveness of any of them. Finally, students and teachers alike will be able to understand the continuity and sequence of the total program since generalizations arise naturally from the content that is studied, as opposed to some of the other criteria, such as expanding environments or chronology, which are superimposed on the content because of their functional utility as convenient devices for articulation.

SUMMARY AND CONCLUSIONS

This chapter has briefly sketched the functions which generalizations may serve in a K–12 social studies program. Hopefully, it has given the reader, whether he be teacher or administrator, some reason to pause and question whether his present social studies program could not be improved by putting some of these functions to work in the near future.

CHAPTER 4

Some Words of Caution About Generalizations

GENERALIZATIONS have certain dangers and limitations to which the teacher should be alert. The very fact that generalizations can serve so many important functions in the K–12 curriculum increases the scope within which the incompetent or unknowing teacher can misuse them. A few words of caution are needed.

First, the teacher must be sure that the particular generalization he anticipates the students will discover from a unit of study can, in fact, be discovered from that content, and, more importantly, merits discovery.

Second, the teacher must realize that his preconceived list of generalizations which students are to discover from the unit's content may not be all the generalizations enclosed in the content, or even the best ones. The teacher must permit students to postulate generalizations which he, himself, had not forseen as discoverable from the unit's content.

Third, the teacher should be very alert to the broadness of the unit and the amount of content it contains, since this will dictate to some degree the number and kinds of generalizations the students will be able to discover. A reasonable guideline to use is to have a unit require about three weeks to cover, and to arrange the learning materials so that a half-dozen or so generalizations can be anticipated. The point being that too many generalizations from one unit will lead to a lack of focus on any of them, and will simply turn into a game where one student after another shouts out that he, too, has just discovered a generalization. Keep the number of generalizations that can be anticipated for any single unit down to a manageable quantity, such as six or seven.

Fourth, the teacher must insist that any statements which students offer as generalizations meet the full criteria of our definition and must be able to have proof cited for them. Also, in this regard, the teacher must be keen to the fact that many of his students will memorize several generalizations as the year's work progresses, and will offer these memorized generalizations for each unit of work, regardless of the content studied. These generalizations will usually be impertinent and the teacher should discard them.

Fifth, and most importantly, the teacher must restrain all tendencies to dictate the generalizations to the class rather than have the student discover them for himself. The teacher must be wary not to give direct hints as to where generalizations are in the content, or what kind of generalization they should be seeking. Moreover, he must continue this restraint when students begin to offer statements purporting to be generalizations, requiring the students to refine the statement until it meets the full criteria set for any generalization. Then students must cite proof and determine if there are any exceptions, before the statement is finally accepted by the teacher as a generalization.

The teacher will find that the language used by his students in expressing generalizations will need refining. In most cases, the students' first statement purporting to be a generalization will be incomplete or impertinent, contain definite referents, and simply lack sophistication. Also, the students will use descriptive words rather than social studies concepts in the generalizations. The teacher should be alert for the opportunity to have the class members synthesize several of the statements offered as generalizations into one or two substantial statements.

The teacher, who uses generalizations as the aim of learning and organizes the learning activities to promote discovery of generalizations, can expect each unit to require two or more days longer than customary; however, if the content of the course is carefully selected, this aim of the course—student discovery of a pre-selected list of priority generalizations—can be achieved. A positive corollary to this problem of greater time being spent on each unit is that more in-depth understanding of the content will result when students begin to use the factual content to derive generalizations and cite proof for them. The end result will be that the teacher will have reduced the amount of material he can cover, but will have increased the in-depth attention given to the content so necessary for learning.

Also, more classroom time will be spent on developing the verbal skill of students, especially their ability to generalize and use social studies concepts. As a result, students will become more aware of expressing their ideas, and avoiding empty slogans, verbalisms, and faulty logic.

A final implication of planning a unit so that students are given an opportunity to discover generalizations is the excitement and charged atmosphere which takes place when the factual content has been mastered and the teacher asks the question, "Who has the first statement they want to offer as a generalization?" Experience in the classroom has convinced the author that students will challenge each other's statements, offer their own as an improvement, and will, in general, be as demanding as the teacher in making sure that the eventual generalization is as near to perfection as possible.

CHAPTER 5

Testing Students on Generalizations

THE TEST ITEMS for generalization which are identified in the following pages, must not be considered by the reader as the only types of test items for our entire methodology, the Interdisciplinary Approach to Generalizations, but only for generalizations. Prior to constructing any test for generalizations, the teacher must be reasonably sure that the students have a good grasp of the unit's factual content.

The test items for generalizations should require the students to use inductive thinking on new and familiar content, to formulate one generalization from a series of statements, to cite proof for generalizations, and to employ deductive thinking by applying a known generalization to other content. Also, in testing students on generalizations, the tests should be cumulative as well as at the conclusion of each unit.

Examples of Test Items for Generalizations

The most important type of test item to determine the proficiency of the students in discovering generalizations is to ask them to inductively reason generalizations from unfamiliar content. The generalizations they are to derive may or may not have been encountered before by the students, and the unfamiliar content may have been taken wholesale from a text or contrived by the teacher. Sample test items follow.

Each of the following passages of content contains at least one major generalization. State a major generalization for each and cite two examples of its existence and operation in some other period, place, or among other peoples.

I. Once France realized the immediacy of a forthcoming war, she adopted trade policies which would increase her self-sufficiency. These policies, however, lost France the great advantages of regional specialization and interdependent trade relations.

A. The generalization is _____.

B. Two examples of its existence and operation in other places, periods, or among other peoples are:

1. _____.

2. _____.

II. Prior to the Japanese invasion of north China in 1937, China was beleaguered with internal warring between the Kuomintang and the Communists. However, once the Japanese threatened to conquer the entire country, the warring Chinese united together against this external threat. This united front, though often strained, managed to see the war end with Japan defeated and removed from the Chinese homeland. With the defeat of the Japanese, the united front collapsed and internal warring redeveloped between the Kuomintang and the Chinese Communists.

A. The generalization is _____

B. Two examples of its existence and operation in other places, periods, or among other peoples are:

1. _____.

2. _____.

A second type of test item for generalizations is to require students to synthesize two or three statements, all of which contain parts of a generalization, into one complete substantial generalization. The test item may appear in this form:

DIRECTIONS TO STUDENTS

Synthesize the following three statements into one significant generalization.

STATEMENT 1.   In industrial societies, there is a tendency for self-sufficiency to disappear.

STATEMENT 2.   The very nature of industrialization requires workers to become specialized in the production of a single item or part of an item.

STATEMENT 3.   Since specialization always accompanies industrialization, it means that one producer must find a market for his own goods and a source for the goods he needs.

ANSWER.   The statements may be synthesized into the generalization _____.

For the benefit of the reader to check himself, the above synthesized generalization would be: *During the process of industrializing, self-sufficiency decreases and specialization increases with a resulting need for an increase in the exchange of goods.*

A third type of test item might be of the following manner:

DIRECTIONS TO STUDENTS

Below are two valid generalizations. Cite content from the unit we have just completed which demonstrates their operation.

GENERALIZATION 1.   A vast supply of labor competing for a limited number of jobs has a depressing effect on wages and employment conditions.

The unit content which will substantiate the above generalization is _____.

GENERALIZATION 2.   In organizing governments, it is imperative that the leader be given sufficient power to carry out his duties, but at the same time be held responsible for the wise use of his powers.

The unit content which will substantiate the above generalization is: _____.

A fourth type of test item for generalizations is to present students with an *Understanding*, a term which is developed further in Chapter Six, and ask them to perform certain removal and substitution procedures which transform the Understanding into a generalization. An example of this transformation process is given in Chapter Six.

The aforementioned examples of test items for generalization could serve the teacher as beginning guides; however, in most instances his own creativity should be the best yardstick for constructing test instruments of this nature.

CHAPTER 6

Concepts and Their Relationship to Generalizations

Social Studies Concepts

EVERY GENERALIZATION contains certain key social studies words or phrases which are called concepts. Some examples of social studies concepts are:

1. Revolution
2. Stratification
3. Balance of Power
4. Diminishing Returns
5. Regional Specialization
6. Productivity
7. Cultural Lag
8. Nationalism
9. Ideology
10. Family
11. River
12. Republic
13. Government
14. Institutions
15. Customs
16. Election

A social studies concept is a word or phrase which has associated with it certain salient, inalienable features. The understanding and proper use of the concept depends on the mastery of the inalienable features as well as the common definitional meaning of the word.

Concepts have both a denotative and connotative level of meaning. The denotative level is simply the dictionary definition of the word. Thus, the denotative meaning of the concept *Revolution* is a rapid change of a procedure, custom, or institution.

For many purposes, the denotative level of meaning is sufficient for proper usage of a word, however, it is not sufficient when social studies concepts are used. Social studies concepts, like concepts from all fields of study, have a connotative level of meaning, and it is this higher level of meaning which our students must be trained to understand.

Using our concept of *Revolution*, the student trained in searching out its connotative aspects would discover that they include all the following:

1. The connotative meaning of *Revolution* embraces the denotative meaning.

2. The concept *Revolution*, unlike revolts or riots, has the features of being organized and planned.

3. The concept *Revolution* implies leadership, either by a small group or by an individual.

4. *Revolution* has the inalienable feature of beginning, with rare exceptions, as a minority movement or in a subordinate position.

5. *Revolutions* always have the feature of being opposed to something, whether it be a person, an event, or an institution. Moreover, Revolutions not only oppose something, but they are, themselves, always opposed either by the installed powers or by other different revolutionary groups.

6. Once the *Revolution* is successful, the viewpoint of the revolutionaries toward other different revolutions is not unlike the viewpoint once held by the previously installed power toward the now successful revolutionaries.

These connotative features of our concept, *Revolution*, must be understood before anyone can completely grasp the full meaning of a Revolution, whether it be the American Revolution, Russian Revolution, revolutions in manufacturing, or what have you. All social studies concepts have connotative features which students must be given an opportunity to discover. It seems foolish for the teacher to assign students to study the French *Republic*, the Common Market's *regional specialization*, the rate of *economic growth* in the U.S.S.R., or Africa's *underdeveloped nations* until the students have a fair grasp of the connotative features of any republic, regional specialization, rate of economic growth, or underdeveloped nation.

Failure to understand the connotative aspects of concepts has led to ridiculously empty verbalisms, such as describing the Cold War as a war being fought at the North Pole, or defining a communicable disease as one able to be talked about.

Teaching Concepts: The Process of Concept-Formation

The process of teaching the connotative aspects of concepts is called concept-formation. This process requires introducing students to concepts over long periods of time in varied settings so that the student will discover for himself the diverse connotations of the concept. This indicates that it is incumbent on each teacher to seize every opportunity to introduce students to a new concept, to probe their minds for the inalienable features they associate with the concept at the time it is introduced, to correct mistaken connotations, expand on valid connotations, and to give students an opportunity to see the shades of meaning of different but similar concepts.

Concepts, like words with only a denotative meaning, are best taught when the usual rules of vocabulary development are observed.

1. The concept should always be introduced in a context rather than in isolation. Preferably, the first introduction to the concept should be in two or more contexts which reveal the concept's different shades of meaning.

2. Students should be given an opportunity to arrive at their own meaning of the concept prior to guidance and direction from the teacher. Students' discovery of the many and various connotative features of social studies concepts will increase their understanding, use, and retention of the concepts. One of the best methods of helping students to arrive at their own meanings of

concepts is by asking them to substitute concepts for descriptive words. Thus, in the generalization "A *division of labor increases the efficiency of the workers so they can produce more goods in the same or a lesser period of time,*" the student can substitute the concept *productivity* for all the descriptive words following the verb "increases." Thus the generalization would read: "A division of labor increases *productivity*." In the process of arriving at the concept *productivity* both the teacher and students had opportunities to discuss why other words, such as manufacture, produce, production, output, and quality were not acceptable and how they differed from the concept *productivity*. A search for the correct concept heightens the students' awareness of concepts, and the eventual discovery adds significance to them.

3. In concept-formation students should perform reading, listening, and writing operations on the concept as soon as it is introduced. The psychology of learning tells us that using the senses of seeing, hearing and speaking concurrently increases our grasp and retention of any knowledge.

These three guidelines for concept-formation should, of course, be followed by test items which will measure how well the students understand and apply the concepts. Again it is necessary to point out that in any test for our entire methodology, the Interdisciplinary Approach to Generalization, concepts would be only one of several types of test items.

Test Items for Concepts

Test items to measure the students' understanding and use of concepts can include all the following:

1. Students should be required to substitute the correct social studies concept for a group of descriptive words. An example is the use of the concept *productivity* as shown above.

2. Students should be required to choose the proper concept from several similar concepts or words. For example, they would choose the concept below which best completes the statement,

When a country attempts to insure that neither of several other countries gain the upper hand over each other, we say the first country is practicing the technique of _____.
    (a) separation of powers,
    (b) balance of power,
    (c) division of power, or
    (d) checks and balances.

3. A more exacting type of concept test item ties concepts to content. Examples of such test items are:

A. The political science concept of *Balance of Power* is best illustrated by _____.
    (a) efforts of Theodore Roosevelt in arranging the Treaty of Portsmouth;
    (b) U. S. selling wheat to the U.S.S.R. in 1964;
    (c) Gentleman's Agreement;
    (d) JFK's stand against a hike in prices by the U. S. Steel Corporation.

B. The sociological concept of *Ethnocentrism* is best revealed in practice by _____.
    (a) countries which have no restrictions on immigrants,
    (b) the melting pot idea about the U. S.,
    (c) the apartheid policy of South Africa,
    (d) interracial marriages.

C. The economic concept of *Regional Specialization* is best revealed by _____.
    (a) Germany's efforts to produce its own oil during World War II,
    (b) the Common Market,
    (c) a policy of self-sufficiency,
    (d) the trading of identical products by two or more countries.

4. A fourth type of test item for concepts would simply be to require students to identify social studies concepts, assign the concept to its appropriate social science discipline, and list several connotative aspects of one or two selected concepts.

In summary, the process of concept-formation requires the introduction of the concept in one or more contexts; the use of the senses of seeing, hearing, and speaking; the comparison of shades of meaning of the concept with other concepts and words; and the testing of the students' general understanding and use of the concepts.

The Relationship of Concepts to Generalizations

Generalizations and concepts are best learned when their interdependence is capitalized on and their differences are kept clearly in mind. The major differences between generalizations and concepts are as follows:

1. Generalizations are principles or rules expressed in a complete sentence, whereas concepts are not principles and are expressed in a word or phrase.

2. Generalizations have a thesis; that is, they indicate something about the subject of the sentence. Concepts have no thesis.

3. Generalizations are objective and impersonal and have a thesis which is not contestable, whereas concepts are highly personal and subjective and may have connotative aspects which vary from peoples to peoples. Thus, the concept of Revolution may have the varying connotative aspects to different peoples of being a good thing or a bad thing, an unlikely event or an inevitable event, and so on.

4. Generalizations have universal application, whereas concepts are usually limited to particular peoples with fairly similar languages who apply similar connotative meanings to the concepts. Certainly, the concepts of *Peace* or *Liberation* do not mean the same for Americans as they do for the Chinese or Russian Communists. Concepts also have limited application simply because many of them, such as *cultural lag* or *profit motive*, are unknown to other peoples. Also, concepts have limited application even within a time period, since the connotative aspects of any concept changes over a period of time

just as the meaning of words change. Certainly the concept of *Capitalism* has connotative meanings today that it did not have in the days of Adam Smith.

These differences clearly indicate that generalizations and concepts are two different things; however, they do not point out the excellent educational benefit of combining the two into one methodology. Generalizations, as complete sentences, may and should contain one or more concepts; however, concepts, as words or phrases, can not possibly contain a generalization. We can readily see how it would be possible for a teacher to introduce concepts while studying or formulating generalizations and to follow-up the introduction by the process of concept-formation which was outlined previously. It is not so readily perceived how a concept, essentially its connotative aspects, can help to formulate a generalization.

We have already indicated that every social studies concept has a denotative and connotative level of meaning, and that understanding the latter was essential for social studies. To repeat a point made earlier, the connotative meaning is nothing more than the salient, inalienable features which a person associates with the concept. These connotative aspects of social studies concepts can frequently, though not always, be combined to form a generalization which meets all of our criteria. Examples will illustrate this point. It is entirely possible to combine the connotative aspects of the concept Revolution into the generalization, *Revolutions are organized, led and always opposed, and when successful take on a viewpoint toward other internal revolutions not unlike the viewpoint held by the previously installed group.*

The connotative aspects of the concept, *Division of Powers*, would include:

(1) that at least two or more units of government exist;

(2) that each unit has some particular powers which the other units do not have;

(3) that when there is a conflict or overlapping in the use of particular powers, one unit of government will be recognized to be superior to the other units;

(4) that there is some validity to the maxim that "power corrupts, and absolute power corrupts absolutely."

These connotative aspects can be combined into the generalization, *the possibility of democracy is increased and dictatorship decreased when the powers of government are divided among governmental levels to prevent concentration of power in the hands of one level of government.*

Teachers must be alert to all possibilities of introducing concepts into the formulation of generalization, training students to develop skill in concept-formation, and helping students to combine the connotative aspects of a concept into generalizations.

In Chapter 3, it was suggested that the teacher should determine the generalizations which his students might discover from each unit of study for the year's course and then use the generalizations to select and organize the course content. In this chapter, the reader was introduced to the great value of mastering concepts, both intrinsically and for learning generalizations. We can now suggest that when the teacher has decided on the anticipated generalizations the student will discover from each unit of study, he then identify the key concepts contained in these generalizations and outline the connotative aspects of each, so that when students engage in the process of deriving generalizations from the factual content, the teacher will be prepared to ensure that specific concepts are included and that concept-formation can take place on these specific concepts.

Thus, the tenth grade teacher's planbook for a particular unit on the Industrial Revolution might have the categories shown in Table 6.1.

Understandings: Their Relationship to Generalizations

Before the conclusion of this section on generalizations and concepts, it is necessary to introduce a new term which is both

Generalizations and Concepts in the Teacher's Planbook

A 10th Grade World History Unit on *The Industrial Revolution*[a]

TABLE 6.1.

Major Content (Understandings) Students are Expected to Learn	Anticipated Generalizations to be Discovered by Students (Important Concepts are Italicized)	Connotative Aspects of Italicized Concepts
1. That industrialization refers to changes of production from handicraft to machinery; from the home to the factory; from local markets to national and world markets.	A. The problems and demands imposed upon a society's education system increases as that society engages in the *process of industrialization*.	A. Process of industrialization 1. 2. 3.
2. That the favorable results of the Industrial Revolution included: (a) the availability of better and more goods for all,	B. *Governments*, to remain in existence and be effective, must be responsive to the changing conditions and demands of the people.	B. Governments 1. 2. 3.
(b) the development of great cities and urban centers, (c) the promotion of reforms in agriculture and science, (d) the appearance of new classes with an eventual growth of democracy,	C. The *self-sufficiency* of the family decreases as the process of *division of labor* in the *factory system* increases.	C. Self-sufficiency 1. 2. 3. Division of Labor 1. 2. 3. Factory System 1. 2. 3.
(e) new impetus for women's rights, (f) the appearance of labor unions to protect the rights of workers,	D. *Supply and demand* for various categories of labor will produce wage differentials, which in turn leads to class stratification.	D. Supply and Demand 1. 2. 3. Class Stratification 1. 2. 3.

TABLE 6.1 *(continued)*

Major Content (Understandings) Students are Expected to Learn	Anticipated Generalizations to be Discovered by Students (Important Concepts are Italicized)	Connotative Aspects of Italicized Concepts
(g) eventual social legislation to protect workers, children, and women and promote social betterment, (h) the rise of humanitarian movements, (i) the rise of industrial empires, (j) the eventual increase in time available for recreation and education. 3. That the unfavorable results of the Industrial Revolution included: (a) the creation of slums resulting in decline of health and moral standards, (b) poor labor conditions with numerous accidents and great insecurity among workers, (c) widespread exploitation of women and children,	E. *Patterns of consumption* vary as income changes.	E. Patterns of Consumption 1. 2. 3.
	F. *Industrialization* demands *specialization* which in turn must be accompanied by a growth of exchange and trade.	F. Industrialization 1. 2. 3. Specialization 1. 2. 3.
	G. As an *industrial society* matures, more time is available for *recreation* and *leisure*, which become social problems if left unattended.	G. Industrial society 1. 2. 3. Recreation and leisure 1. 2. 3.
	H. The existence of *humanitarian groups* in a society is evidence of unsolved problems in that society and man's concern for those hurt by such problems.	H. Humanitarian groups 1. 2. 3.

TABLE 6.1 *(continued)*

Major Content (Understandings) Students are Expected to Learn	Anticipated Generalizations to be Discovered by Students (Important Concepts are Italicized)	Connotative Aspects of Italicized Concepts
(d) breakdown of rural family life leading to social and political problems such as rotten borough system,	I. Man's *longevity* is strongly influenced by his *standard of living*.	I. Longevity 1. 2. 3. Standard of living 1. 2. 3.
(e) industrial warfare between labor and management, (f) development of radicalism including anarchy,	J. In a *free market system*, the price of an article is a reflection of the relationship of the supply and demand for that article.	J. Free Market system 1. 2. 3.
(g) growth of imperialism and colonialism, (h) development of an industrial society plagued by cycles of recession and depression, (i) loss of personal pride in the produce of one's labor. (j) erection of trade barriers in the form of high protective tariffs,	K. During the process of producing any given commodity, a point of *diminishing returns* is reached wherein each additional unit of production has a higher cost of production.	K. Diminishing returns 1. 2. 3.

a The author acknowledges the efforts of Mr. Bert Gardner of the Wyandanch School District, New York in the preparation of the information represented in this table.

intrinsically valuable and important for discovering generalizations. Recently, several state education departments have prepared social studies content outlines which include a summary of the major content thoughts or outcomes which the students, hopefully, should have mastered from a particular unit. These major content thoughts are being called Understandings.

An Understanding is one or more summary statements containing the major thought or idea in a passage of content or teaching unit. It usually has definite referents of time, place, and people and is unmistakenly derived from the body of content just studied. Its *immediate* applicability is solely and directly related to that content and no other.

An Understanding for a seventh grade unit which had centered on the various reasons for the development of New York City as a major commercial and trade center might be:

New York City developed as a major commercial and trade center because of its natural geographic advantages, including harbors, and ports suitable for large trading vessels; outlets on major bodies of water; proximity to markets; a productive hinterland and others.

The New York State Education Department, Bureau of Social Studies, has done some very important pioneering work in identifying, formulating, and applying Understandings in some of their syllabuses. In a 1965 tentative syllabus, *Social Studies: Grade 7: Our Cultural Heritage, Grade 8: United States History*, they indicate their criteria for Understandings as:

"Each Understanding should be important to itself and should have specific reference to the topic.

Each Understanding should contribute to a broader generalization that has application at many points in the social studies sequence.

Each Understanding should include words, or phrases, that bring to mind mental images or concepts. These images, or concepts, which constitute the specialized vocabulary of the social sciences, will acquire broader and deeper meanings as pupils

meet them at successive grade levels in increasingly sophisticated contexts."

This tentative syllabus then outlines how these criteria for
Understandings might appear when applied.

"To illustrate the application of these criteria, we may use an
Understanding from eighth grade United States history which
could be stated as follows:

"The United States, in the first four decades of its history,
had great difficulty in trying to maintain its neutrality in a
world dominated by the British-French power struggle."

This, in the judgment of the syllabus committee, is an important Understanding. It has specific reference to a topic being
studied. It contributes to broader generalizations which could
reads.

"Weaker nations are likely to experience difficulty in maintaining neutrality (or non-alignment) in a world dominated by a
struggle between great powers." or "The first responsibility of
any government to the nation it rules is the survival of that
nation."

These broader generalizations have had many applications and
are highly pertinent to world conditions today. As for the mental
images or concepts that appear in this Understanding, the two
most obvious are "neutrality" and "power struggle." If pupils
have never heard these terms before, the concept-building will
begin here. If they have met the terms in othr contexts, the
study here should give new depth and dimension to the concepts or mental images the terms represent.

An Understanding from eleventh grade American History might
be:

"Advisors other than members of the cabinet have frequently
played key roles in presidential decision-making."

It has specific reference to the topic of the executive branch of
government. It contributes to this generalization:

"Many administrators who have heavy responsibilities rely upon
personal and confidential advisors for help in decision-making."

In the case of this Understanding, it is doubtful that pupils will meet new mental images or concepts, but older images that may be reinforced and broadened are "cabinet" and "presidential decision-making."

The State Education Department, after noting that the first two steps in using the syllabus are to assemble teaching materials and to plan the learning experiences, asserts that, "The third step in using this syllabus is to determine the correct use of the Understandings and related content. The Understandings stated in each syllabus are not facts to be taught; they are goals to be reached. If pupils merely learn to repeat these statements verbally or in writing, without first laying a foundation by the exploration of related content—reading, observing, inquiring, forming hypotheses, making intuitive surmises, testing the hypotheses, becoming aware of the tentative nature of many "answers"—they will acquire only empty verbalisms, to be parroted and forgotten. Topics should not, therefore, be introduced by giving pupils copies of the Understandings."

After describing how Understandings can be introduced and how students can be encouraged to go beyond the stage of simply acquiring information, the tentative syllabus indicates that, "In the process of reaching those Understandings that are pertinent to the topic at hand, students, especially in the senior high school, can be guided in the formulation of related generalizations. They can also be led to find new meanings in the special words and phrases of the social science vocabulary, the mental images, or concepts."

The remainder of the tentative syllabus is comprised of topics for grades seven and eight. These topics are outlined in three parts. The first part is the Understanding, which is immediately followed by the content from which the Understanding was discovered and formulated. The second and third parts usually consist of a few lines entitled GENERALIZATIONS and CONCEPTS, respectively.

Thus Topic 3 of the eighth grade section of the tentative syllabus is entitled The Age of Jackson (1825–1840's). Some of the Understandings which students should learn from the content of the unit are:

THE FIRST POLITICAL MANIFESTATIONS OF SECTIONAL DIFFER-
ENCES BECAME APPARENT, FOLLOWING THE ERA OF GOOD FEEL-
ING, IN THE ELECTIONS OF 1824 AND 1828.

IN THIS PERIOD, THE ABUNDANCE OF WESTERN LAND SERVED
BOTH AS A CONTRIBUTOR TO THE RISING TIDE OF DEMOCRACY
AND AS A SOURCE OF FRICTION AMONG VARIOUS ECONOMIC
GROUPS.

DURING THIS PERIOD, POLITICAL DIVERSITY WAS CLOSELY TIED
TO SECTIONAL INTEREST.

"EXCEPT FOR JACKSON'S CRUSADE FOR THE COMMON MAN AND
POLK'S FOR TERRITORIAL EXPANSION, MOST POLITICAL CAM-
PAIGNS (1825–1850) WERE FAIRLY INDECISIVE.

Topic 3 is concluded by the sections on GENERALIZATIONS and
CONCEPTS.

"A few sample generalizations that might be derived from Topic
3 and later tested for validity in other contexts:

Transplanted communities tend to preserve but make adjust-
ments in the institutions they know.

Records as war heroes have been assets to candidates for high
elective office.

Inventions are often delayed in their development while the
science and technology upon which they depend catches up
with them.

A few sample concepts that might be introduced or deepened
in Topic 3:

Caucus	Nullification
Cession	Reform
Debtor	Temperance

Additional generalizations and concepts should be developed
by the teacher and class as they work on Topic 3."

The Bureau of Social Studies and the curriculum development bureaus of the New York State Education Department
have done a masterful job in compiling and organizing the

factual content, Understandings, generalizations, and concepts in this tentative syllabus. Certainly, they would be the first to recognize that much more needs to be done. In particular, there is a desperate need to show the exact methodological steps a teacher might use to develop generalizations from Understandings.

It has already been stated that Understandings are intrinsically valuable since they comprise the major content thoughts of the unit. They are also valuable as a content source from which generalizations can be discovered and formulated. This does not mean that every Understanding, with a few verbal additions and omissions, can be transformed into a generalization. It does mean, though, that some Understandings contain the crux of a generalization and can be readily made into a generalization. When an Understanding does lend itself to being changed into a generalization, the process might simply be one of removing all the definite referents and substituting, if necessary, more encompassing words, so that the contrived generalization has unlimited application.

For example, our Understanding about New York City which was referred to on page 41 stated that:

New York City developed as a major commercial and trade center because of its natural geographic advantages, including harbors and ports suitable for large trading vessels; outlets on major bodies of water; proximity to markets; a productive hinterland and others.

By applying the process of removing all definite referents, we can transform this Understanding into the generalization,

Major commercial and trade centers are located where one or several natural geographic advantages exist, including harbors, ports, proximity to markets, productive hinterland, and others.

The process of removing definite referents and other limiting terms to transform an Understanding into a generalization is not applicable to many Understandings. Consider the impossibility of transforming the following Understanding from Topic 3 of the New York State Education Department's Tentative Syllabus on Social Studies, Grades Seven and Eight.

"EXCEPT FOR JACKSON'S CRUSADE FOR THE COMMON MAN AND POLK'S FOR TERRITORIAL EXPANSION, MOST POLITICAL CAMPAIGNS (1825–1850) WERE FAIRLY INDECISIVE.

The process of transforming Understandings into generalizations where applicable, would seem to be a very important procedure for introducing students to generalizations for the first time; for primary and lower elementary grade students; and for students unable to apply inductive thinking to the degree required for the discovery of generalizations. However, for other students, especially those of average or above ability, the teacher would hopefully expect the students to discover and formulate generalizations outright, rather than employing the transformation process.

SUMMARY

This chapter, which concludes the first section of this book, has concerned itself with concepts, their definition, their process of formation, and their relationship to generalizations. It has also focused on Understandings, particularly how they are valuable for purposes of formulating and discovering generalizations. Students should be expected to arrive at the important Understandings of the content of each unit, and where possible to use those Understandings as sources of discovering generalization, either by outright discovery or, where applicable, by applying the transformation process of removing definite referents and limiting words. In this process, the teacher must be wary not to de-emphasize the Understanding because of the anxiety of students to proceed to the generalization; or to do so much substitution and removal from the Understanding that the generalization in no way can be said to be derived from or supportive of the Understanding. Finally, the teacher and students must keep clearly in mind that many Understandings simply cannot be transformed into generalizations by any process whatever.

CHAPTER 7

An Interdisciplinary Approach to Social Studies Content

Its Advantages and Implications

THE PRECEDING CHAPTERS have been devoted exclusively to generalizations, and to a lesser degree, concepts and understandings. All have been defined, their characteristics noted, their advantages and limitations identified, and their interrelationship stressed. These three elements are interrelated goals of instruction which indicate where the teacher and his students should be headed, but they don't indicate very much about *how* they get there.

The interdisciplinary approach does, however, lay out a path which will take the teacher and students toward these instructional goals. The interdisciplinary approach is not only a path to generalizations but contains a variety of assets which, themselves, should be important goals of instruction. The two most outstanding assets of the interdisciplinary approach are: (1) its value for developing the ability of students to understand and use the great and unavoidable interrelationship of all the social sciences in grasping a comprehensive picture of a single body of content, and (2) its value for providing students with opportunities to develop the ability to make sophisticated use of the skills and techniques of the social sciences.

An interdisciplinary approach refers to the concurrent use of two or more social science disciplines to study the same content.

For too long our students have been asked to view all social science content from only geographic and historical perspectives; and it might be said that even when the perspectives were restricted to these two disciplines, the students still were not asked to use the tools and skills of the historian or geographer. They were simply asked to learn what had been put in print. This travesty of providing students with the time dimension of history, and the place dimension of geography, and calling the outcome learning should not be allowed to continue. Where are the other social sciences and the vitality and comprehensiveness which they would add to our field?

The social sciences are geography, history, political science, economics, sociology, anthropology, and social psychology. Each has as its focus the study of man and his institutions. Each makes use of many common skills and techniques; and yet each has its own specific skills and techniques for studying its particular realm of the broad category of man and society.

Each of the social sciences share the identification of, and use as research guidelines, the major principles and generalizations of the disciplines; the use of scales and symbols as devices for representation; and the use of statistical formulae and data to substantiate inferences and hypotheses.

Just as all social science disciplines share common skills and techniques, each has its own particular version of skills, techniques, and ways of knowing which make it unique in its approach to content.

The discipline of economics can be used to illustrate the uniqueness of each of the social sciences. First, the particular concern of all economics in the broad study of man and society centers on how societies have tried to meet the problems of a scarcity of goods and the exchange of these goods. These problems of scarcity and exchange are the sources from which emanate the problems of the economist, and they give direction to his thinking as he runs through the maze of details and facts which characterize and confuse his work. Absorbing questions which guide his search for answers are of the type: "What goods are needed or desired, how available are they, and from where?"

In approaching economic problems, he designs technical words, such as gross national product, rate of economic growth, and capital formation, which have a precise meaning to him, and which he uses in a precise manner. He assigns specific traits to these technical words and develops a system of relationships among the economic factors which these words describe. Thus, he will have a system of relationships such as:

(1) supply and demand schedules, (2) Gresham's law, (3) quantity theory of money, (4) productivity and the combination of input factors, and (5) a nation's resources and its population growth.

He has developed graphs, models, and statistical methods to represent economic factors and their interdependence. Economic texts bulge with charts, graphs and statistics representing balance of payments, purchasing power, real wages, gross national products and hundreds of other topics.

Each of the social science scholars has developed similar sophisticated ways of approaching his content, and has honed tools and techniques to analyze the content and facilitate decision-making.

The interdisciplinary approach asserts that the teacher must *not* restrict the student's perspective of social studies content to history or geography, but must bring to bear on the content all applicable disciplines. Of course, it is certainly recognized that a few units in any course of study are best studied by only one discipline. What disciplines of the social science could you apply to a unit entitled, *A Study of the Topography of North America*, except the discipline of geography? Fortunately a dull unit, such as the title of the one above suggests, should be a rare instance when the interdisciplinary approach is employed.

Thus, the interdisciplinary approach would say to the teacher preparing to teach a fifth, eighth, or eleventh grade unit from American History—for example, let us say the unit is one on immigration to the U. S.—go ahead as usual and give the time and place dimensions of immigration by using the disciplines of history and geography, respectively. These two disciplines should help the students understand:

1. when the various waves of immigration occurred,

2. the historical reasons for the waves of immigration,

3. the countries from which the immigrants came and the areas of the U. S. where various nationalities settled, and

4. their contributions to the development of our society.

It is at this point that the teacher usually stops, considering the unit completed. The interdisciplinary approach would now urge the teacher to give students an opportunity to view immigration from one or more of the perspectives of sociology, anthropology, economics, and political science.

Using one or more of these disciplines, in addition to geography and history, the students might, for the very first time, be exposed to such information,

1. From anthropology and sociology as:

(a) the old world cultures of major immigrant nationalities, the introduction of concepts of tradition-directed societies, patriarchal and matriarchal societies, and others;

(b) anthropological differences of nationalities;

(c) social classes represented by various nationalities, the introduction of concepts of social class, social stratification, achieved and ascribed status, and others;

(d) social problems experienced by immigrants in the United States, and the social problems caused by immigration;

2. From economics as:

(a) skills, wealth, and education of various nationalities:

(b) effects of immigrants on labor unions, United States industrialization, location of business enterprises, and others;

(c) effects of immigrants on United States acquisition of territory and settlement of the frontier;

3. From political science as:

(a) the type of government which existed in the immigrants' native country;

(b) the philosophies of government brought to the United States by immigrants, the introduction of concepts of anarchism, radicalism, Fourierism, and Fabianism;

(c) government problems caused by immigrants, both in domestic and foreign affairs.

In the first or second grades, an interdisciplinary approach to the study of the home might have all of these aspects.

A First or Second Grade Unit on the Home

The study of a home from a geographic approach would answer the following questions:

(1) Why do people build homes where they do?
(2) Why are homes shaped differently in various parts of the community?
(3) Where is the home located in relation to a major city, the school, the surrounding communities, surrounding states, the region?
(4) What materials are used to build homes and from where do they come?

The study of a home from an economic approach would answer such questions as:

(1) Who owns and who builds homes?
(2) Are homes expensive? Where do home owners get the money to buy homes?
(3) Why do some people have small homes and some luxurious homes?
(4) What machines are used to build homes?
(5) What craftsmen are needed to build homes?

The study of a home from a sociological approach would answer such questions as:

(1) Who lives in homes? Why do we need homes?
(2) What rooms of the home are set aside for special purposes?
(3) What do mothers do in homes? Fathers? Children?
(4) How is living in a house different from an apartment?

Our unit on homes could also be studied from the perspective of political science, history, and anthropology. The important point is for the teacher to have the students study the topic from the perspective of several disciplines, and thereby increase their understanding of the many facets of man and institutions.

The interdisciplinary approach, by bringing together the interplay of the social science disciplines, opens a vista for students to see a more comprehensive picture of man and society.

The Interdisciplinary Approach and the Skills of the Social Sciences

An integral part of the interdisciplinary approach is the skills and techniques of the social sciences. Skills and techniques are not to be left to haphazard chance but are to be specifically identified and taught in each unit of study. The interdisciplinary approach asserts that the social studies teacher, not unlike the mathematics teacher, must devote classroom instructional time to developing the ability of students to use the skills of the field, and this should be a continuing phase of the entire course of study.

In the primary and lower elementary grades, many of the skills students would be introduced to, and would develop some competence to use, would be general and not strictly limited to the field of social studies. A typical list might include such general skills as:

1. locating information from books, encyclopedias, reference sources, dictionaries, newspapers, magazines, indices and guides;

2. gathering facts from interviews, field trips, and audiovisual materials;

3. using maps and globes;

4. organizing information into outlines, major ideas, pertinent and impertinent data, opinion and facts, and summaries;

5. learning how to read and listen for specific purposes;

6. developing a social studies vocabulary and communicating ideas;

7. interpreting pictures, charts, cartoons, tables and other types of representation;

8. learning to work in a group setting by accepting responsibilities and working harmoniously with others to achieve common goals.

During these early school years, the student should be as concerned with learning general skills as with learning particular social studies skills. However, when a student reaches the upper grades, he should be ready for some rather sophisticated skills and should spend an ever-increasing amount of time on social studies skills, as opposed to general skills. He could be expected to develop a competence with social studies skills such as:

1. evaluating social studies source materials based on established criteria; as having students establish their own criteria to evaluate biographies and then applying this criteria to one or more books;

2. establishing a criteria for the geographer's concept of "region" and constructing a fictional region having realistic areal relationships among its parts;

3. substantiating written information by preparing statistical graphs and drawing inferences from their data, and explaining the process of thinking by which the inferences were derived;

4. locating a passage of content demonstrating the historian's use of interpolation or extrapolation, and developing a criteria which the author might have used to make his hypothesis.

Of course, these skills are sophisticated and have strong implications for the unsure or incompetent teacher. The teaching of sophisticated social studies skills offers the competent instructor an opportunity and challenge to be creative as well as develop his own technical skills.

SUMMARY

The two distinctive aspects of an interdisciplinary approach are: (1) the concurrent use of two or more social science disciplines on the same content, stressing the particular focus and "ways of knowing" of each discipline, as exemplified with the discipline of economics, and (2) the teaching of social studies skills in a systematic pattern and as an integral part of each unit of study.

For the classroom teacher the interdisciplinary approach has important implications. He must increase his own understanding of each social science discipline, particularly those other than history and geography. He must record in his planbook the specific skills he intends teaching in each unit, and he should prepare and have on hand lists of library resources for himself and his students which are valuable for skill development.

CHAPTER 8

An Interdisciplinary Approach to Generalizations

THE FIRST SEVEN CHAPTERS have set down the nature of social studies generalizations and an interdisciplinary approach. This chapter unites the two elements together into the interdisciplinary approach to generalizations, and shows the teacher, whether she be at the kindergarten or senior high level, the structure of model units based on the approach. The author hopes teachers will study the model units very carefully and then attempt to draft and use their own units in the classroom.

A Skeletal Outline of Model Units for the Interdisciplinary Approach to Generalizations

Title of Unit   Grade Level

I. Descriptive Statement
II. Provocative or Leading Question(s)
III. Suggested Disciplines (Interdisciplinary)
IV. Specific Skills to be Developed
V. Answers to the Provocative or Leading Question(s)
VI. Content Sources
   A. Books and Periodicals
VII. Generalizations to be Discovered. Citations of Proof.

I. Descriptive Statement

The descriptive statement characterizes the unit of study, often pinpointing the focus of the unit. We have purposely omitted from the statement any philosophical slant or value judgment. An example of a descriptive statement is:

> "This unit is a study of the role of urban civilization in the predominantly rural and agrarian society of colonial Amercia."*

On occasion the descriptive statement may indicate the thesis of the unit, such as:

> "The process of industrialization, as experienced first by England and later by many other nations, enabled millions of people to lead richer and healthier lives, yet confronted society with difficult problems of adjustment, some of which still perplex us."*

II. Provocative or Leading Questions

A teacher can direct the students' attention to the next content to be studied by using films, reading a poem, telling an anecdote, referring to a quotation, or simply presenting a picture or replica of an event. Any of these can be used with the interdisciplinary approach to generalization, however, there is still a great need, even after students have been motivated, to focus their attention directly on a specific topic or part of the content, rather than all the content. Probably, the simplest and most effective method of doing this is to begin the unit with a question, particularly one of the "how or why" variety. Such a question forces the teacher to choose the topics to be studied, to decide what is to be learned about the chosen topic, and frequently suggests the disciplines most valuable for pursuing the answers to the question. A unit of study based on the interdisciplinary approach to generalizations may have more than one provocative or leading question, or may have one major question and one or two related minor questions.

The broadness of the question has important implications for

---

*1965 *BOCES Social Studies Report.* Board of Cooperative Educational Services, Huntington, New York.

the amount of content to be taught in the unit, the time to be spent on the unit, and most importantly, the number and kinds of generalizations to be derived from the content. In general, the teacher should avoid unusually broad questions, and try to formulate questions which are concise and to the point.

The following examples of provocative questions illustrate their multifacet functions.

Provocative Question for a Third Grade Unit on Communities

Using your present community and a colonial village as examples, how would you demonstrate the belief that a person's physical environment is very important for the way he makes a living and how well he lives?

Provocative Question for an Eighth Grade Unit on Thomas Jefferson

How did the needs and desires of Napoleon Bonaparte and Thomas Jefferson in 1803 make them natural trading partners for the Louisiana Territory?

Provocative Question for a Tenth Grade Unit on The Industrial Revolution

"How is the process of industrialization such that the favorable and unfavorable results experienced by England were also experienced by most other industrializing nations?"

III. Suggested Disciplines (Interdisciplinary)

A provocative question suggests the social science disciplines that are employed in seeking the answers to the question. An example of a provocative question is *How were the location and development of colonial cities a result of their natural advantages?* In pursuing the answers to the question the student needs to use the skills and techniques that characterize geography, economics, political science, and history. In the interdisciplinary approach, two or more disciplines must be used concurrently on the same content, hopefully with the result that students will see the interplay of the social science disciplines, and will gain a more comprehensive picture of the content.

IV. Specific Skills to be Developed

As an intrinsic part of the interdisciplinary approach, the teacher must identify and make plans for students to use the skills which are needed to answer the provocative question. Whenever possible, students should be referred to library sources where he can find explanations and examples of specific skills. The teacher can also compile a list of sources to refine his own skills, or to demonstrate the application of certain skills to the class members.

V. Answers to the Provocative or Leading Question

In his planbook, the teacher should summarize the answers to the provocative question. Often, these summaries are called Understandings. The summary should not be interpreted by anyone as the full extent of the factual knowledge students can learn from an interdisciplinary study of the content, but only as the gist of that learning. These factual answers along with other learning then become the sources which students will probe for generalizations.

VI. Content Sources

In his planbook, the teacher should list any content sources which would be valuable to the class member or himself in answering the provocative question.

VII. Generalizations to be Discovered. Citations of Proof.

The planbook should include those generalizations which the students will most likely discover. The generalizations should be carefully worded, just as the teacher hopes the students will finally formulate them.

For example, in a study of Sub-Saharan Africa during the ninth grade, the student will no doubt be exposed to the fact that:

By most standards the Africans are considered to be illiterate, economically and culturally backward, and by some standards might even be considered uncivilized. Most of the Africans, however, do not see themselves this way.

In trying to formulate a generalization from this factual statement, the students may indicate that outsiders and visiting observers do not have the same view of peoples or cultures as the inhabitants. From this the teacher might ask if other peoples see the people of the United States in the same way that we view ourselves. At this point, it is quite likely that some students will perceive that the people living in a country have a different view of themselves and their culture than outsiders because each uses their own values, mores, and standards to evaluate themselves and each other. Thus, the generalization, "Man views all people, including himself, in terms of his own *cultural mores, values, and standards."*

The process of drawing generalizations is one the teacher must guide, constantly questioning the statements offered as generalizations, and requiring their refinement until the statement is, in fact, a generalization. The generalization should arise naturally from the content of the unit and should not be superimposed or extraneous. The number of generalizations will vary with each unit, but will usually be a function of the broadness of the provocative question. The kind of generalizations, that is, the social science discipline that they are a part of, is even more a function of the provocative question, as are the skills used in answering the question. It is generally expected that most, though not necessarily all, the generalizations will come from the social science disciplines identified under the category, *Suggested Disciplines.*

The concepts contained in the generalizations should be underlined, and their connotative aspects outlined.

Once the class has offered a statement, which the teacher and class members tentatively accept as a generalization, the class is then asked to cite historical examples that would bolster the belief that the statement is, in fact, a generalization. For example, the generalization, *"Specialization encourages each region to produce those goods which it can produce most efficiently thereby leading to increased interdependence among trading regions,"* could be substantiated by offering such proof as: cotton culture of the Southern States of the United States prior to the War between the States, the premises behind the formation of the European Common Market or the Outer Seven, and the cultivation of sugar in the Caribbean Islands. If any exception can be cited which disproves the statement, then it is immediately disqualified as a possible generalization.

In any unit, there will be some generalizations which are of better quality and more pertinent than others. In most lengthy units, the teacher may not find it possible to have proof cited for all the generalizations. In such cases as these, the teacher should stress those generalizations which he deems most important for that unit and those that correlate most with the suggested disciplines. Thus, if the suggested disciplines for the unit were economics, geography and sociology, then generalizations from these disciplines would be stressed.

A Model Unit

We now choose a unit of study and show how the various parts of the interdisciplinary approach to generalizations appear. Our example is a unit on immigration which might be taught at grades 5, 8, or 11. In this case, we are considering an 11th grade unit.

Title of Unit

The Immigration Policies of the United States   *Grade II*

I. Descriptive Statement

The descriptive statement indicates in a simple and concise manner the content of the unit.

This unit is intended to give the students a broad viewpoint of American immigration policies and particularly to show how the policy changes made following World War I really divided U. S. immigration policy into two distinctive contrasting eras: (1)

From colonial days to World War I, when there was no general immigration restriction and only slight restrictions against specific nationalities, particularly the Chinese and Japanese. (2) From 1921 to 1965 when there was general restriction on all nationalities, but more restrictions on some nationalities than on others.

II. Provocative or Leading Question

The descriptive statement indicates to some degree the focus of the unit, but the provocative question will periscope the attention of the students on a specific aspect of the general topic of U. S. immigration.

Why did the U. S. Government change its immigration policy following World War I?

III. Suggested Disciplines (Interdisciplinary)

This provocative question suggests that students pursue the factual answers by using the disciplines of history, geography, sociology, and political science.

IV. Specific Skills to be Developed

In this stage of the methodology, the teacher must identify in his planbook the skills which students should employ in ferreting out the factual answers to the provocative question. He should also include a description of the way in which he will introduce students to the social studies skills needed in this unit. Thus the teacher should have a list of sources which students might use to understand and apply certain skills.

In this particular unit on immigration, students might be asked to understand and use the following skills:

(1) Each class member would be asked to choose library sources which would help to answer the question; to offer reasons why he chose the sources he did and omitted others; to outline the organization of the source if it is an index or reference book; to identify any limitations of the selected sources; and to identify the bibliographic tools he used to locate the sources he intends to use.

(2) Each class member would be asked to identify and summarize the immigration laws prior to World War I and to do the same for laws following World War I.

(3) Each class member would be asked to compare and contrast the two sets of laws, noting their major similarites and differences. They should also be asked to compile their own criteria for the ways in which the laws were similar and the ways they were different.

(4) Each class member would be asked to prepare a bar graph and a broken-line graph showing the changing number of immigrants of each nationality that entered during selected periods or years. Students would be required to choose the most important nationalities to be included, and decide on the periods of immigration to be represented.

(5) Each class member would draw conclusions and make inferences from the statistical data on the graphs.

The teacher might ask questions such as the following:

(a) Which nationality has the greatest percentage increase in immigration between 1860-1920; 1920 to 1960; which had the smallest percentage increase for the same periods?

(b) For every Italian that entered the U. S. between 1900–1920, how many of each of the following nationalities entered?

> How many Germans?
> How many French?
> How many English?

(c) What percentage of all immigrants that entered between 1920–1960 were English? Russian? Hungarian?

(d) If the rates of immigration for each nationality remain the same for 1960–1980 as they were from 1920 to 1960, how many more Russians will enter than Hungarians? More Irish than Bulgarians? More French than Italians?

(6) Each student would be asked to establish a cause and effect relationship for the immigration laws passed following World War I.

In the interdisciplinary approach to generalizations, each skill is discussed during class and the teacher includes skill development as an integral part of the unit.

V. *Answers to the Provocative or Leading Question*

Thus far, our provocative question has caused the students to focus their attention on a specific topic of immigration and to use the skills of certain social science disciplines. The use of the skills was required and arose naturally from a pursuit of the factual answers to the provocative or leading question. In the daily lessons, the teacher has arranged his instructional methods and materials to ensure that the students have a fair grasp of the factual answers to the orienting question. It is important for the reader to observe that the interdisciplinary approach to generalization does not dictate the day-to-day teaching methods the teacher uses, but it does help him to select, organize, and arrange his methods and materials to enhance the achievement of his instructional goals, namely the discovery of generalizations by students.

Though our methodology does not dictate instructional methods or materials on a day-to-day basis, it does ask that each teacher observe three guidelines.

1. The content which the students are to learn must contain strands or parts of the generalizations which the teacher anticipates students will discover. The teacher can assure this by his daily selection of topics for class discussion or homework, outside reading assignments with summaries, and audiovisual materials.

2. Students should be asked to write summary passages of the major thoughts or ideas of the content which contains the strands or parts of generalizations. These summaries would be similar to what we earlier described and identified as Understandings.

3. Prior to any attempt whatsoever to have students attempt to discover generalizations, the students should have taken examinations which confirm their reasonable understanding of the facts of the unit.

In this particular unit on immigration, it can be expected that the students would offer the following factual answers to the provocative question.

1. Many Americans believed the new Communist government

in the U.S.S.R. was sending its immigrant agents (Comintern) to our country to infiltrate our labor unions and social groups and to establish their own political party for the purpose of subverting the U. S. Government. This belief led to hysteria and irrationality on the part of many Americans, which historians have labeled The Red Scare.

2. Many Americans believed the New Immigrants had ideals and political theories which were alien and dangerous to our democracy. The failure of these "New Immigrants" to be integrated into our society (acculturation) was often submitted as proof that they had no desire to become Americans.

3. The "New Immigrants" caused our major urban centers many perplexing social problems of housing, education, and health and posed serious problems for the labor unions. The peoples affected by these problems along with many vested interest groups called for an end to immigration.

4. The restrictive immigration policy following World War I was just one more aspect of the general isolationist foreign policy that the United States adopted following the disillusionment with the war and the Treaty of Versailles.

These factual answers in conjunction with the other factual content the students learned in the unit become the source for our generalizations.

VI. Content Sources

VII. Generalizations to be Discovered. Citations of Proof

From the mass of facts learned, the students should attempt now to discover if there are generalizations which can be made concerning man and society. This requires inductive reasoning, the perceiving of universals from a vast collection of particulars. This step of the approach might begin with the teacher asking the class, "Are there any generalizations which you have learned from this unit which apply to other peoples, places, or times?" This type of question is designed to encourage the students to begin offering statements which they feel are generalizations. Each worthwhile statement is written on a chalkboard, and the students are encouraged to examine it for defects, suggest modifications, expand on it, reword it, or discard it. This process involves the students to a man, and the teacher might find he is rather superfluous in this "tearing apart" process. This process should continue until the class finally agrees that the refined statement does, in their opinion, meet the full criteria of a generalization.

During the process of formulating a generalization, the teacher will have many opportunities to encourage the students to use social studies concepts rather than descriptive words. The teacher should seize each of these opportunities and ask the class to select the concept which best meets the requirements of each generalization. If the concept is a new one for the students or one about which the teacher feels they still have doubts, he should lead the students through the stages of concept-formation. This means that the teacher must have recorded in his planbook, as part of the generalizations, the concepts he expects students to use and the connotative aspects of the concepts he intends to stress.

In our unit on immigration, the anticipated or unanticipated generalizations the students might have discovered from the factual content could include all of the below.

1. The amount of *status* and prestige conferred on various groups in society reflects the priorities and values of that society.

2. *Cultural ethnocentrism* reveals itself when man views all people, including himself, in terms of his own *culture*.

3. The *process of acculturation* is carried on by many *societal agencies*, but primary of the agencies in all societies is the family.

4. All societies have the problem of instilling *values* and goals in their members which ensure the performance of necessary tasks.

5. The more industrialized and complex the society, the more the society relies on formal, rather than informal, institutions for maintaining *social control*.

6. People tend to immigrate to, and find success in, physical environments most closely resembling those from which they came.

7. Every culture attempts to maintain itself by transmitting its values and mores to the young.

8. Conditions in the physical environment of a region influence the relative density of human population.

9. Traditional patterns of life are highly resistant to even minor change.

10. The interrelationship of man and his physical environment has contributed to diverse cultural development.

11. Though there are variations among individuals in terms of race, religion, and nationality, these variations do not necessarily imply inequality.

12. All peoples of all cultures have produced symbols which convey their values and tell something about their way of life.

13. People often follow customs and habits, long after the reasons for their coming into being have disappeared.

14. Each generation of a society modified its heritage to meet its own needs.

15. Government, to remain in existence and be effective, must be flexible in meeting the changing demands of the people, though the demands may be irrational as well as rational.

16. A vast supply of labor competing for a limited number of jobs has a depressing effect on wages and employment conditions.

17. The supply and demand of various categories of workers brings about wage differentials and social stratification.

The number and kinds of generalizations in any unit will be a function of the amount of content required for study to answer the provocative question. In general, the broader the provocative question, the more generalizations the students will discover. Though there is no magical number of generalizations, experience indicates that six to eight for a three week unit seems reasonable. The author has included seventeen generalizations in the model unit solely for illustrative purposes.

The teacher should always be alert to possibilities of synthesizing two or more inferior generalizations into one very substantial one, and to the fact that some generalizations though valid in every respect, are nevertheless impertinent for the particular unit under study.

The final step in the interdisciplinary approach to generalizations follows the students' agreement that a statement they have offered is a generalization. The teacher does not accept any statement as a generalization and neither should the students until proof is cited which shows the existence and operation of the generalization in other places, times, or among other peoples. Also, the statement will not qualify as a generalization if a significant exception can be cited.

The citation of proof stage of our methodology has several commending features. First, it asks the students to consider their experiences and knowledge, to analyze them, and to determine their suitability as proof for the generalization. Second, it is an opportunity to reinforce previously acquired knowledge and to use that knowledge in support of a generalization. Third, it provides a natural means of transition from events of the past to events of the present. It gives students a chance to see how the past and the present are interlocked, when they understand how a generalization derived from content about the past can now be substantiated by an event of today. In this regard, it permits current events to be brought into the classroom in a meaningful manner and helps to answer the perennial student question, "Why should I study something that happened long ago?"

In our unit on immigration, the students might have cited as proof for the generalization, *Governments, to remain in existence and be effective, must be responsive to the changing demands of the people, though the demands may be irrational as well as rational,* any of the following:

1. The failure of the Articles of Confederation was due primarily to their inability to meet the needs of the time, such as controlling interstate and foreign trade, providing uniform and stable currency, and maintaining stability at home.

2. When Charles I failed to liberalize the government and make peace with the Protestants, the Stuarts were overthrown by the Puritan Cromwell.

3. The continued existence of the American Government under a constitution more than 175 years old can be traced to its

changing character through the amending process, congressional legislation, judicial decisions, and customs.

Eight other model units for selected grade levels have been included in the appendices. These model units deserve close study by those teachers who anticipate employing an interdisciplinary approach to generalizations. It is also important for the teacher to keep in mind that all the model units in this publication have been prepared for the teacher, and thus the vocabulary level of each part of the format, including the generalizations, reflects the reading ability of the intended reader rather than students.

CHAPTER 9

A Plan of Action for Developing a K–12 Social Studies Program

THE PRECEDING PAGES contain the rather simple premise that the teacher of social studies, whether primary, elementary or secondary, should introduce his students to the techniques and skills used by *all* social scientists, and these tools and techniques should be focused on content with the purpose of students discovering the generalizations and concepts of the field.

The model unit on immigration is one way the teacher could organize his lesson plans to achieve the above objectives. It is not the only way, and may not even be the best way. The individual teacher can best make that judgment. The important step is for the teacher to accept or reject the premise. That being done, the procedure of developing units to incorporate the premise is an organizing rather than theoretical challenge and can be attacked by a formal plan of action.

A Plan of Action for Social Studies, K-12

For those social studies teachers and school systems which accept the premise above and want to incorporate it into their K–12 social studies program, the following plan of action will be valuable.

Preliminary Steps in the Plan of Action

I. All teachers, K-12, who instruct in social studies should have made available to them a sampling of the literature which pertains to the premise. Specific literature which should have priority would include:

Berelson, Bernard and Steiner, Gary A., *Human Behavior: An Inventory of Scientific Findings.*
Bruner, Jerome, *Process of Education.*
Elam, Stanley, *Education and the Structure of Knowledge.*
Hanna, Paul R. and Lee, John R., "Generalizations from the Social Sciences," (Social Studies in Elementary Schools, Michaelis, John U., ed., 32nd Yearbook of NCSS.).
Turner, Gordon B., ed., *The Social Studies and the Social Sciences.*

The teachers should agree on the definition of terms. Several examples of generalizations, concepts, understandings, an interdisciplinary approach and skills should be made available for discussion.

II. With an individual copy of defined terms and examples in hand, groups of teachers would begin to prepare written materials.

A. The social science teachers with the best academic preparation and experience should prepare a comprehensive list of generalizations for each discipline. Thus, for the discipline of economics there might be as many as 50 priority generalizations. These generalizations would be in their most abstract form, complete, and in no way repetitious of each other.

Some priority literature which would be very valuable in preparing these generalizations would include the following, all of which have rather extensive lists of generalizations.

1. *Report of the State Central Committee on Social Studies to the California State Curriculum Commission,* State Education Department, 1961.

2. Stanford Social Studies Research Project under Professors Paul R. Hanna and Richard E. Gross. (This is a very extensive list of generalizations as compiled by ten doctoral students and would probably be the best source. It is im-

portant to know, however, that many of these generalizations need refinement and synthesis.)

3. 1965 Social Studies Summer Workshop Report of the Board of Cooperative Educational Services, Third Supervisory District, Deer Park Road, Huntington, New York.

B. Each abstract generalization would then be formulated into a degree of complexity and completeness—without losing the thesis—where it would be appropriate for students at various staggered grade levels. Thus, for every generalization there should be prepared a chart showing its appropriateness in terms of complexity and completeness for such grade levels as 1, 3, 5, 7, 9, and 11.

C. Other teachers should prepare a list of key concepts, designating the grade level at which the student could be expected to have a knowledge of the concept. The best way to compile such a list is to review the basic textbook used at each grade and take note of the key concepts at the end of each chapter. Sometimes the key concepts are already identified in the teacher's annotated edition of the textbook.

D. There should also be prepared rather extensive charts on skills. These charts should include skills which are a shared responsibility of social studies and skills which are uniquely those of the social sciences. The skills charts should indicate the grade level(s) where the skill would be introduced, refined, and extended. For the most part, the chart should follow the pattern established by Eunice Johns and Dorothy McClure Fraser in the 33rd Yearbook of the NCSS, pages 310–327. Another valuable resource is the 1965 Social Studies Report of the Board of Cooperative Educatinal Services, Huntington, New York, which contains many examples of social studies skills.

E. Descriptive outlines of each social science discipline should be prepared. The outlines should contain:

1. a general description of the discipline, particularly its main concern in the broad realm of man and society, its distinctiveness from other social science disciplines, and its particular viewpoints and methods of examining and organizing content; and

2. sample lists of the major concepts, generalizations, and distinctive skills of each discipline.

In preparing these descriptive outlines for each social science discipline, some very valuable reference literature would be:

Anderson, Howard R., et al., *High School Perspectives*.

Meyerhoff, Hans, ed., *The Philosophy of History in our Time*.

Turner, Gordon, et al., *The Social Studies and the Social Sciences*.

F. A small group of teachers should prepare sample test items to demonstrate how students' knowledge of concepts and concept-formation, generalizations and their application to new situations, and Understandings might be evaluated. Most of the test items might be of the types described in this book. A model test for one specific unit for selected grade levels might be very valuable for illustrative purposes; that is, a model test for a specific unit of the seventh grade social studies course.

G. There should be prepared descriptions of "suggested methodology techniques" showing teachers some of the techniques which have been found to be valuable in helping students to discover generalizations and form concepts.

A section devoted to discovering generalizations should include many of the procedures brought out in this book. These would include:

1. Insuring that the content containing the generalizations is given due emphasis in class, and that the classroom activities are put in a sequence which helps the students to recognize a common principle at work in a variety of situations.

2. Having students summarize the major points or events which transpired in the order in which they took place, and to postulate a generalization based on the sequence of events without reference to specifics of the particular events under study.

3. Having students state Understandings, and then by the transformation process described in this book, change the

Understanding into a generalization, if possible.

4. Having students develop techniques for the inductive thinking process. These are not easy to teach; however, much can be done to alert students to search out generalizations by providing them with some of the ground rules of induction. The process of inductive reasoning can also be enhanced by making students aware of relationships among phenomena. These relationships are often expressed as: cause and effect; inverse and proportional; cumulative; cyclical; temporal; events in series; multiple causation and effects, and others. Many of these relationships can be demonstrated to students by using inferential thinking, which, of course, is an intrinsic part of the inductive process.

This section on generalizations should also include many classroom hints as to the teacher's reaction to a proposed generalization from the class; his manner of requiring them to formulate it completely, asking them to cite exceptions to it and cite proof for it. There should also be some description showing how a generalization, once learned, can be used to learn other facts; that is, the deductive value of generalizations.

Included in this section on suggested methodology techniques should be a brief review of the denotative and connotative aspects of all social studies concepts and the concept-formation techniques outlined in this book.

H. Finally, several units should be prepared, not necessarily or even preferably having the same format, demonstrating how the various parts of the interdisciplinary approach to generalizations are interrelated and how they should all be provided for in each instructional unit. This format need not and probably should not be as formal as the illustrative unit format on U. S. Immigration. Hopefully, however, the format would give proper attention to *all* the social sciences, their skills, concepts, generalizations, and understandings.

All of the information gathered should be compiled into individual booklets and made available to "experimental teachers."

The Experimental Stage

The experimental teachers should consist of all those who participated in the preparation of the booklet, and others who might volunteer, or the administration might ask to assume such responsibility. The important criteria for the experimental teachers is that they enter into the experiment willingly, and that they have some orientation, preferably in-service training, prior to using an interdisciplinary approach to generalizations. The organization of the experiment teachers should meet at least these requirements:

1. There should be at least three teachers from each grade level, who are teaching the same social studies subject.

2. Every school building should have at least three or more of the teachers; however, they should not all be teaching the same grade level.

3. None of the teachers should be first year teachers, or experienced teachers who are teaching a subject for the first time.

4. The experimental teachers at grades 7–12 should not try to teach all of their classes in the experimental manner, but should teach at least two classes, both of which are taking the same social studies subject.

5. A central office administrator should be the coordinator of the experimental teachers, though not the chairman of operational meetings, in order to ensure the availability of working space, materials, and the necessary time.

6. The observation and/or evaluation of the experimental teachers must be carried out in a totally nonpunitive manner. Preferably, the experimental teachers would be permitted and encouraged to conduct class intervisitations, and to impersonally analyze and criticize each other's proficiency with the methodology.

7. If possible, the experiment should begin at the opening of the school year or at midterm. Also, once the teacher has begun to use the interdisciplinary approach, he should stay with it for the remainder of the school year and use it consistently.

8. It is preferable to limit the initial experiment to teachers of advanced and regular students, rather than having it apply to below average students. Later, of course, when the results of the experiment have been evaluated, the district's teachers should employ the interdisciplinary approach on a total basis.

Once the experimental teachers have been selected and organized, and with the booklets on hand, the tryout phase of the interdisciplinary approach to generalizations should be initiated. This tryout phase should focus on these objectives or functions:

1. As the experimental teachers prepare the format for each unit, they should compile bibliographic sources for both content and skills from the individual school or district library. Thus, the first unit at the fifth grade might be *The Natural Features of the Western Hemisphere*. During the planning of the unit, the teachers would compile a short list of the books and materials on hand in the school and district libraries which might be useful for teaching the (1) content of the unit and (2) the skills which the students will employ in studying the content.

At the end of the experimental year, there should be available for each grade level and every social studies subject a composite bibliography of local sources for both content and skills, unit by unit.

2. As the experimental teacher prepares his units, he will indicate the concepts to be identified and the generalizations likely to be discovered. During the teaching of the unit, other concepts and generalizations will come from the students which the teacher had not anticipated, but which he will want to add to his unit plans for future use.

These concepts and generalizations would be compiled into composite lists, with each unit of each subject taught having specific concepts and generalizations which the teacher should anticipate students would discover.

Thus, at the end of the experimental year, a school district would have composite lists available for each unit of each subject. These lists would be of four types:

1. A list of skills to be developed in each unit and a bibliography of local library sources which will help the teacher and/or students to learn the skills.

2. A bibliographic list of local sources available to teach the content of each unit for each subject K–12.

3. A composite list of concepts to be identified and developed (concept-formation) for each unit of each subject. Ideally, there would be several key concepts from each subject of each grade level which would have the connotative aspects clearly outlined in this composite list.

4. A composite list of all generalizations to be discovered for each unit of each subject, preferably with the wording used by the students and accepted by the teacher during the experimental year.

Whether there would be a composite list of examinations given during the experimental year at the completion of each unit is a decision best made by the experimental teachers and the administration. Certainly, it would be valuable to have various types of test items for concepts and generalizations compiled and made available for illustrative purposes.

As a result of the experimental year, a school district would have in compiled form what would be virtually a *suggested* course of study for each social studies subject at every grade level, K-12. Individual grade level booklets should be assembled and made available to all teachers of social studies, following in-service training.

During the experimental year and thereafter, the district should have a standing committee of teachers which would carry on continuous evaluation of the methodology and synthesize the information derived during the experimental year. This committee should also spend considerable time in perfecting testing instruments on a grade level basis, and to develop ways and means of implementing the methodology for below average academic students.

SUMMARY OF THE PLAN OF ACTION

Preliminary Steps

1. Acquaint teachers with the literature pertaining to an interdisciplinary approach to generalizations.

2. Prepare the following materials:

(a) A list of priority generalizations for each discipline in their most abstract form.

(b) Formulate these abstract generalizations into appropriate degrees of complexity and completeness for students at such staggered grade levels as 1, 3, 5, 7, 9, and 11.

(c) A list of key concepts for each grade level, with several illustrative examples of the process of concept-formation.

(d) A skills chart indicating the grade levels when each skill should be introduced, refined, and extended.

(e) A brief descriptive outline of each discipline showing its distinctive generalizations, concepts, and skills. This outline is designed to introduce teachers to all of the social science disciplines, and to encourage them to make use of each of them, rather than rely solely on history and geography.

(f) A list of sample test items and model tests for illustrative purposes.

(g) Some "suggested methodology techniques" to aid the teachers in instructing students to use inductive thinking, discover generalizations, and form concepts.

(h) Several model units which teachers can use as models in preparing their own units.

The information outlined in Steps 2a-h should be compiled into individual booklets and made available to the experimental teachers.

Experimental Stage

1. Choose the experimental teachers carefully, and follow the organizational principles suggested earlier in this chapter. The experimental teachers should have some brief in-service training.

2. As a result of the experimental stage, the district should have on hand the following composite materials which would constitute a suggested course of study for social studies, K-12:

(a) The units comprising each social studies course which were developed by the experimental teachers. Thus for grade one, each of the three or more experimenting teachers would have prepared a dozen or so units during the experimental year. These 36 or so units would be synthesized and would constitute a unit-by-unit development of the first grade's course of study. This same process is equally applicable to the other grades.

Each of these units would have at least the following component parts:

(1) A list of skills to be developed in each unit with a limited bibliography of local library resources which would be valuable to master each skill.

(2) A bibliography for each unit which would be valuable to master the content of the unit.

(3) Lists of concepts and generalizations discovered in each unit.

Implementation and Follow-up Stage

1. During the second semester of the experimental year, the in-service training of the other social studies teachers should begin. In most cases twelve hours of intensive training are adequate to prepare teachers to use the interdisciplinary approach with some degree of sophistication.

Once the teachers have completed the in-service training, they should be given the materials which comprise their grade level's course of study and asked to make consistent use of them.

2. A standing committee of teachers would carry on continuous review of the interdisciplinary approach during the implementation stage. In particular, it would be carefully attuned to the feedback of all teachers and make changes where necessary.

A Comparison of the Schools of the Present and Past

GRADE ONE

I. Descriptive Statement

The school has always been a place for young people to learn under the guidance of a teacher. The school of today is vastly different from the school of our early history, in its size and design, the number of teachers and other working people in it, and its modern furniture and equipment. Its purpose, however, remains the same; to provide an education for its young students.

II. Provocative or Leading Question

In what major ways do our schools of today differ from the schools of our early history?

III. Suggested Disciplines (Interdisciplinary)

1. Geography   2. Sociology
3. Economics   4. History

IV. Specific Skills to be Developed

A. Students will be asked to prepare a map or sketch indicating the location of the school in relation to certain other places; the home, the closest store, the fire station, police station, and town hall. They will be asked to develop a mileage scale indicating the respective distances of each of these places from the school, and to choose a symbol to represent each place, including the school. In this skills activity, the students should be introduced to place concepts, such as: near, far, close, and distant, and such directional concepts as south, north, east, west, up, down, parallel, and perpendicular.

B. Students will draw a sketch of their own school, labeling the location of major areas such as classrooms, playground, library, principal's office, cafeteria, major entrances and exits, and the gymnasium. Their location and direction in relation to each other should be labeled by cardinal directions of east, southeast, southwest, northeast, and so forth.

C. Prior to discussing the ways in which schools have been financed, ask students to consider the following questions: (The teachers should be alert to the fallacies in his thinking including impertinent answers, incomplete answers, failure to consider implications of the answers, failure to consider practicality of the answers, and others.)

1. Should everyone pay for the costs of our schools?

2. Should everyone pay the same amount?

3. How should we determine the amount each person should pay?

4. If everyone does not pay the same amount, what is the best way to decide the amount each person should pay?

5. What might be some disadvantages of having the amount of school taxes each person pays depend on the value of his property?

D. Students would be asked to interpret information.

1. Picture information could be presented by cartoons, films, and slides. Students would be asked to tell what they see, the relationship among the various parts of the visual information, and what these relationships mean.

E. Students should learn time concepts such as minute, hour, day, week, year, decade, century, future, past, ancient, modern, before, after, now, meanwhile, and long ago. Students might also be asked to put these time concepts into a sequence ranging from the most recent to the most distant past, as: now, seecnd, minute, hour, day, week, month, year, decade, and century.

V. *Answers to the Provocative or Leading Question*

Schools of the present are different from schools of the past in these major ways:

A. In their appearance and construction:

The school of the past was usually a one room converted store or barn. It might have one or two windows which provided all the light available. The room was often made of logs held together by twine and mud plaster. Heat was provided by a pot-belly stove or an open hearth. Students brought their food, usually eating it at their hardwood desks. There was no library, gymnasium, or any other building except the classroom itself. Schools of the present usually have many rooms, including those which are used as libraries, gymnasiums, cafeterias, and offices. Schools are often more than one story high, having a bottom floor basement which provides centralized heating. Schools of today are most often made of brick or some type of masonry, often in bright colors. The children eat their lunch in modern cafeterias, have playgrounds to play on, and have access to many books in the library.

B. In the number and kinds of people who work there:

Schools of the past were usually manned by one individual, who did all the many jobs required for schools. He provided the wood for heating the one room school, brought drinking water to the students from the nearby stream or well, and served the students as teacher, counselor, and disciplinarian. More often than not, the teacher was not trained or experienced at teaching but had simply taken the position out of interest or necessity.

Schools of today are much larger in size and the number of students who attend. They need many professional people to offer a good education. Teachers, who are well-trained and often experienced, provide the students with the instruction and help needed at each grade level, while the principal helps the teacher to make the best use of his time by arranging his teaching schedule and by handling the many administrative problems of discipline, community relations, and finances. Others, such as the school nurse, the counselor, custodian, cafeteria worker, and safety patrol policemen, help the principal and teachers to carry out their job of educating the youth of the community.

C. In the ways in which money to pay the costs of running the school is obtained:

Schools of the past depended heavily on the people of the community for money to run the school, just as is done today. However, in the past the only real expense was the money paid to the teacher and the cost of firewood and possibly a book or two for the students. Not all communities had the same rules for the people who were to pay taxes or how much they were to pay. In some communities only those with children in school paid taxes, while in others everybody paid. Often the parents paid a certain amount for each child in school, while in some communities everybody paid the same amount regardless of the number of children they had in school. Parents were often permitted to pay their school taxes by giving to the teacher such items as wood, tobacco, credit at the local store, or even food.

Schools of today depend on the people living in their school district for the money to support the school. In general, this money is paid in the form of taxes. Though the taxes might be state taxes, sales taxes, or commercial taxes, the major source of taxes are those put on the private property of the community members. Usually each person's home and land is determined to be of a certain value by an assessor, and then a particular tax rate is applied to it. This means those with valuable property pay more school taxes than others, though all property owners must pay regardless of whether or not they have children attending school. The local government and the school authorities cooperate closely on deciding on the expenses of the school and the ability and willingness of the people to meet the expenses.

D. In the type and manner of education the student receives:

In schools of the past, the education centered on students learning to do the "three R's" and they often learned the "three R's" under great pressure from the teacher. In general, students did not talk in class except to answer the question of the teacher. Usually students were asked to memorize a certain poem, phrase, or paragraph and then to stand and recite it to the class. Great importance was given to mastering fine details of spelling, writing, and arithmetic, and to putting the details into one's memory to be recalled in the future. Students usually had one book and this was the only source of learning except for the teacher. There were, of course, no films or slides, and only occasionally were maps or globes available. Discipline was quite harsh and rather frequent, and of course, the teacher's word was law in all cases. Students who received a sixth grade education were rare since it was customary for young students of ten or eleven years of age to leave school and take on a full time job on the family farm or in the family store.

Schools of the present also teach reading, writing, and arithmetic, but they also teach many other things. The student is usually not asked to memorize his school work, but to understand the reasons for the way things are. Often he is asked to question things and to discover the way things are for himself. Students are encouraged to participate in class discussions, to express their views on the story they hear or read and the cartoons and movies they view. Often they have available many types of books, magazines, maps, globes, and visual aids to help them learn, and in addition, they are able to learn not only from the teacher, but from the school nurse, principal, and custodian. The emphasis on discipline and a student's self-control is still very strong, but the punishment is less harsh. Students are encouraged to remain in school for graduation, and every effort is made to make school life a vital part of growing up.

VI. Content Sources

A. Books and Periodicals

BEIM, JERROLD, *Country School*, New York: William Morrow and Co., Inc., 1955.

FOSTER, M. C., *Miss Flora McFlimsey and the Little Red Schoolhouse*, New York: Lothrop Co., Inc., 1957.

HOFFMAN, ELANE, and HEFFLEFINGER, JANE, *School Helpers*, Chicago: Melmont Publishers, Inc., 1955.

LATTIMORE, E. F., *First Grade*, New York: Harcourt, Brace & World, Inc., 1944.

McCREADY, A. B., *A Day at School*, New York: E. P. Dutton & Co., Inc., 1936.

VII. Generalizations to be Discovered. Citations of Proof

A. The need for more and better education increases as the community becomes more modern and industrialized.

B. All communities provide some form of education for the youth.

1. Ask students to identify the educational needs of an Indian youth in past history and to show how they differed from his educational needs today and why.

2. Ask students to consider the educational needs of a person living on a farm as compared with a person living in the city.

C. The construction of a building often indicates the variety of functions carried on in it.

Ask students to make observations on such buildings as a church, police station, fire station, and ball park, and to indicate the way in which the buildings are constructed and why they have a certain shape or certain rooms.

D. When the functions of a school system are divided among people, the functions are performed better and often quicker.

E. Other social agencies beside the school help to educate the youth of the community.

1. Ask students to consider the education they receive from their church leader and officers; their parents and rela-

tives; their older brother or sister; the neighbors; and local policemen.

F. Schools, like other *social institutions,* have changed in response to the changing needs of the people.

G. The *value* of an education is not restricted to the person himself, but is valuable for the community as a whole.

   1. Ask students to consider the value of a doctor, church leader, teacher, or policeman to his community.

H. When the amount contributed to a social agency depends on the *wealth* of the community, it can be expected that some communities will have more and better social agencies than others.

   1. Ask students to compare the amount of money which might be available to be spent in his community for social institutions as compared with (a) a nearby community, (b) a farm community, (c) a large city.

I. Though *money* does not guarantee the success of a social institution, it does make it possible to avoid some of the defects which often lead to failure.

J. The more *primitive* or *agrarian* the community, the more the education of the youth rests with the *family* rather than a *public school.*

The Newspapers of Our Community

GRADE TWO

I. Descriptive Statement

Every community depends on the printed word, as well as other forms of communication, for information and news about local and distant events of current interest. People of the community want to know what and why major news events are happening in their own community, in the United States, and throughout the world. In a democracy, communication and information are essential to the smooth operation of government and business, since it is the people's opinions which help our government and business leaders to make decisions.

II. Provocative or Leading Questions

What is a newspaper and how is it produced? What are its advantages and disadvantages as a form of communication as compared to television?

III. Suggested Disciplines (Interdisciplinary)

1. Economics   2. Sociology
3. Political Science

IV. Specific Skills to be developed

A. Students should prepare an interview questionnaire to be used in interviewing a local official or newsworthy person. They should arrive at decisions as to the types of questions permissible in an interview; the appropriate length of an interview; the right of the person being interviewed to simply say "no comment" and the requirements that the questions be concise, pertinent, and able to elicit the desired answers.

B. Have the students describe verbally or in writing an event in the classroom where no words are spoken. The teacher and one or two students could plan a series of actions in which emotions, facial expressions, gestures, and physical movements were evident to the class. The students would be asked to describe exactly what happened. This type of exercise is very valuable to teach students:

1. The importance and dangers of drawing inferences about an observed event by relying on the expressions of the participants in the event. Here, there would be an opportunity to examine the process of drawing inferences, its necessity and its drawbacks.

2. The importance of tracing events in proper sequence.

3. The difficulty and dangers of establishing a cause and effect relationship when observing an event or person, such as when the students see the teacher and *think* he is angry at a student; the student then goes outside the classroom. Did the teacher cause the student to leave the room?

C. Ask the students to list all the aspects and operations involved in printing a story in a newspaper, and to organize them in the sequence of their occurrence. These aspects and operations might include:

1. The news event; a reporter interviewing and writing the story; a photographer making pictures of the event; editing of the story; typesetting; layout; printing; bundling the papers; distribution; store or home delivery.

D. Have the students study one or more pictures or cartoons in the newspapers. Ask them to identify the people and objects in the picture and any relationship among them. Ask them to draw inferences from the picture and to explain how they arrived at the inference.

V. *Answers to the Provocative or Leading Questions*

A. A newspaper is a printed form of communication which attempts to inform people of current events. Some newspapers are dailies, while others are weeklies. Some have only a few pages and sections, while others might have 100 or more pages, and more than a dozen major sections. A newspaper usually contains many pictures with captions to dramatize the written stories. Most newspapers usually contain all the following sections: headlines and lead articles; business, finance, and stock reports; editorials, many of which are syndicated; society pages; entertainment; and advertisements. There may also be human interest stories, topical stories, continuation stories or articles, and cartoons. Some communities have their own newspapers in addition to major newspapers, while other communities depend exclusively on newspapers produced in the cities or adjoining towns.

B. A great number of people and processes are involved in the production of a newspaper. When a newsworthy event occurs in the local town or nearby area, the newspaper dispatches a reporter to the place of the event. The reporter observes the event or its aftermath, interviews witnesses, and attempts to acquire as much information as possible about the event. Often he will have to use files of the newspaper, town hall, library, or police headquarters to get the necessary information to write the background or history of the news story. Once he has the necessary information, the reporter returns to his desk, types the story, and submits it to a superior, often the editor, who may ask that the story be changed to fit into the total organization of the newspaper. The editor will give directions as to whether the story should be shortened, extended, rewritten, or simply eliminated. The story, along with any accompanying photographs, is then sent to the press shop. Here, the typesetter chooses the correct metal letters needed for the story, while a layout man designs exactly where in the total newspaper this particular story will be placed. Once the typesetter and layout man have done their jobs, the printers operate the press machines which will imprint the type on the paper. The printed sheets are then folded into newspaper style, bundled, and made available to the distributor. The distributor, usually a trucking firm, takes the bundled newspapers to local stores and to central drop-off points. Local newsboys then take the number of papers they need and deliver them to the customers on their route.

C. Comparison of Newspapers and Television as Communication Media

1. Advantages of Newspapers

Newspapers are more likely to include local news and human interest stories, and they can be read and reread as often as desired. Moreover, they can be retained for reference purposes. Reading the newspaper is an active process involving the reader. Often, editorials and topical news events of the newspaper become discussion topics for the entire family. Pictures dramatize the stories, while cartoons and human interest stories show the light side of daily life. As a form of communication, newspapers are usually reliable and accurate in their presentation. They are inexpensive and conveniently available to most people.

2. Advantages of Television

Television often makes the news item available to the viewer as it takes place or soon thereafter. The viewer is able to see the event himself and to apply his individual interpretation to it. For the illiterate, and poor reader, it is their best source of information and news. For the busy executive, a five minute news program will help to keep him abreast of major news events of the day. The schedule of television programs is available in advance, thereby making it possible for the viewer to arrange his schedule to that of the particular program he wants to see. Also, many television panel and discussion shows are available to present editorials on the controversial issues of the day. For most Americans, a television set is inexpensive enough to permit purchasing, and is found in the vast majority of American homes.

3. Disadvantages of Newspapers

The news is often a day or so old by the time it appears in the newspaper. Many local newspapers do not cover news events in detail, or have photographs accompanying the major stories. Though newspaper stories are generally reliable, many stories and photographs are often misleading and some are outright fabrications. Some newspapers take a consistent inflexible view of all news and present only this view to its readers. For the illiterate, poor reader, and those with defective sight, newspapers are of little value, unless someone else reads it to them. Though newspapers are available usually, recent labor strikes and the collapse of local newspaper firms, have seriously impaired their availability to some major urban centers and outlying communities.

4. Disadvantages of Television

Though television makes news events available to the viewer almost immediately, this quick service often gives a premature or inaccurate presentation of the news event. Television news programs, themselves, do not usually editorialize but simply report the news. Once a television program is over, there is no means available to see the same program again at a time decided by the viewer. Moreover, the viewer must adjust his time schedule to that of the television schedule, rather than vice versa. Though television sets are relatively inexpensive, there are still many Americans who cannot afford to purchase them, and there are some areas of the country which are still not served adequately by television stations.

VI. Content Sources

A. Books and Periodicals

BUCHHEIMER, N., *Let's Go to a Television Station*, Wisconsin: E. M. Hale and Company (Student Source).

EPSTEIN, SAMUEL, & EPSTEIN, B. W., *The first book of printing*, New York: Franklin Watts, Inc., 1955. A history of printing from the invention of movable type to present-day printing methods which includes an explanation of the three most widely used processes of reproduction—letterpress, gravure and offset (Teacher/Honor Student Source).

NORLING, J. S. & NORLING, E. R., *Pogo's Letter: A Story of Paper*, New York: Holt, Rinehart, & Winston, Inc., 1946. John and his dog, Pogo, visit a papermill and follow the processes of papermaking (Student/Teacher Source).

SOOTIN, L. *Let's Go To a Newspaper*, Wisconsin: E. M. Hale and Company (Student Source).

WEAR, TED, *Brownie Makes the Headlines*, New York: Julian Messner, 1953. An interesting story (for slow readers) of a lost dog is the framework on which is built the description of the printing of a newspaper (Student Source).

VII. Generalizations to be Discovered. Citations of Proof

A. The existence of a free press is one of a country's best assurances of democracy and against dictatorship.

    1. Consider why all dictators would fear a free press.

    2. Consider the advantages of a free press for a democracy.

B. All freedoms, such as freedom of the press, have restrictions on how and when they can be exercised.

    1. A person could not exercise his freedom of speech by jokingly shouting "fire" in a crowded theater.

    2. A person should not accuse another person of a crime or act of misconduct where there is no basis for such charges.

C. To the degree that the national government has silenced the press, it has also impaired one of its best sources of information which might help the government to improve itself.

D. Effective communication usually involves speaker and listener, whose roles may or may not be constantly changing, and the results of the communication should produce a response or stimulate behavior of the people involved.

    1. Ask two of the students to converse, and ask the other students to describe the response of each to the conversation.

    2. Ask the students to consider how they feel when they talk to themselves and under what conditions and for what purposes they do it.

E. Mass communication media (such as television, radio, or newspapers) confer *status*, favorable or unfavorable, on all persons and events it deals with, regardless of the merits of the persons and events.

F. Overcoming communication barriers is a must for other important associations of people to take place.

1. Ask two of the students to "make-up a language" and to use it in conversations with other class members. Ask all the students to analyze the problems that result.

G. All forms of communication are subject to distortion and misinterpretation when they are removed from the context in which the communication first took place.

H. Language and other forms of communication are modified by the listener as he applies his "perception" to the communication.

I. A *division of labor* takes advantage of the skills of the workers, thereby leading to increased *production* and *productivity*.

1. Ask the students to consider how they might go about preparing a newspaper, and why?

A Desert Environment and Its Effects on the People Who Live There

GRADE THREE

I. Descriptive Statement

Of all the places man might make his home, none is less inviting than the desert. A desert life is often one of loneliness, a search for food and shelter, and a constant effort to change oneself or one's environment to weaken the harshness of desert living.

II. Provocative or Leading Questions

What are some of the important features of deserts, and what effects do these features have on life there?

III. Suggested Disciplines (Interdisciplinary)

1. Geography   2. Anthropology
3. Economics

IV. Specific Skills to be Developed

A. Locate the major deserts of the world on a physical map and on the globe. Indicate the latitudes where they are found, noticing particularly the great amount of desert or steppe land between the 15 and 35 parallels.

B. Prepare a bar graph on one or several of the following features of a desert environment:

1. Precipitation
2. Major minerals
3. Population density
4. Diurnal variation of temperature

C. Establish a cause and effect relationship between the climatic conditions and the plant response and/or animal response to these conditions. The cactus and camel would be excellent examples, respectively. Such questions as these might be stimulating:

1. How has the camel responded to the lack of water in the desert environment?
2. What are the advantages of his padded feet and knees in a desert climate?
3. What does the hump of the camel store? Why is this important in a desert climate?

D. Develop an understanding of geographic terms relating to deserts. These terms might include: diurnal variation, temperature, precipitation, relief, oasis, nomad, pastoral nomads, steppe, humidity, climate, domesticated animals, date palms, and nitrates.

E. Ask students to offer reasons for the cause and effect relations of certain areal conditions of physical geography. They might be asked to explain:

1. How the plant life and agriculture of the desert reflect climatic conditions there? These climatic conditions would include light, sporadic rainfall, great extremes in daily temperature, poor quality soils, and high velocity winds with strong gusts.
2. The influence of mountain barriers on trade winds affecting precipitation on both the windward and leeward sides of mountains.

F. Ask students to study any oasis and to cite the various and often ingenious ways in which the people living there have preserved and made maximum use of the scarce water. Such oases as the Nile, Lower Indus Valley, or the Imperial Valley of the U.S. would be excellent examples. In this study of oases, the students should pay attention to such geographic factors as:

1. Location of river streams, usually found in surrounding highlands several hundreds of miles away.

2. Importance of soil and mud deposits made by the river systems.

3. Importance of scarce water for irrigation agriculture, including crops grown during flood seasons such as sorghum and rice.

V. Answers to the Provocative or Leading Questions

A. The important features of a desert environment are:

1. The harshness of the climate for all forms of life. This includes the ever constant lack of water, the blinding winds, the scorching heat, and the general aridity of the area.

2. The effects of the lack of water on plant life, animal life, and human life. Plant root systems probe deep into the soil to gain water, while many animals including the camel and sheep have made biological adaptation to survive in the harsh environment.

3. The existence of a few minerals usually resulting from salt water deposits. These minerals often include sodium nitrates, guano, salt and borax.

B. The important effects of the harsh desert environment on man are:

1. Man has been forced to adapt to the desert environment, and yet he has also been able to change his environment to meet his own needs. Man has adapted to the desert environment in many ways. Some are:

a. He has become nomadic, wandering from place to place in search of pastoral land and water. This constant wandering has forced him to live in easily movable tents and to live on the bare essentials of life. Often the competitive desert life, which is due to scarce resources, has made him a fierce warrior and highly suspicious of others.

Often too, the isolation of his life has led him to become religious.

b. Man has adapted to his environment by wearing white clothes to offset the intensity of the heat, by domesticating animals which he uses for multiple purposes, and by his own self-control in using water.

C. Man has adapted his environment to meet his own needs. Some adaptations are:

1. He has developed many ingenious methods of irrigation to conserve the scarce water and to insure its availability when needed. These methods of irrigation have permitted him to develop an agricultural system on the banks of oases. He has also discovered such plants as the date palm which can thrive in the arid desert climate.

2. He has domesticated animals and found many and various uses for them. They serve him as pack animals, as sources of transportation, protection, food and drink, and often even his shelter is made from animal skin.

3. He has helped to develop mining regions of nitrates, salt, and borax, and even petroleum. Around these mining and industrial regions, villages and settlements have sprung up to serve as commercial villages.

VI. *Content Sources*

A. Books and Periodicals

BEIM, JERROLD, *Eric on the Desert*, New York: William Morrow and Co., Inc., 1953 (1–3). This picture storybook for slower readers about a newcomer's first experience on the Arizona desert provides a good view of the desert and its life (Student/Teacher Source).

CARPENTER, FRANCES, *Our Little Friends of the Arabian Desert*, New York: American Book Company, 1934. o.p. (3–4). Describes the daily life of two children belonging to a Bedouin tribe, and the activities of the tribe through a year of wandering and trading. Stress is laid upon the influence of natural environment on manners and customs (Student/Teacher Source).

DISNEY, WALT, PRODUCTIONS, *Walt Disney's Living Desert* by Jane Warner and the staff of the Walt Disney Studio. New York: Simon and Schuster, Inc., 1955. Goldencraft (1–6) (Student/Teacher Source).

EPSTEIN, SAMUEL, & EPSTEIN, B. W., *All About the Desert*, New York: Random House, Inc., 1957 (4–7). A fascinating report on the deserts of the world with a scientific explanation for their parched state. Includes a description of the plant and animal life inhabiting the desert (Student/Teacher Source).

GOETZ, DELIA, *Deserts*, New York: William Morrow and Co., Inc., 1956 (4–6). An interesting description of desert lands and the plants and animals that inhabit the desert (Student/Teacher Source).

KISSIN, RUTH, *Desert Animals*, New York: David McKay Co., Inc., 1947. o.p. Cadmus. (1–3). A rhymed text and collored illustrations present an attractive picture of life in the desert. For slower readers (Student/Teacher Source).

MALKUS, A. S., *Sidi, Boy of the Desert*, Holt, Rinehart & Winston. 1956 (5–7). An absorbing story of a Bedouin boy and his search for his Arabian colt. A good picture of desert life. (Student/Teacher Source).

PATCH, E. M. and FENTON, C. L., *Desert Neighbors*, New York: The Macmillan Company, 1937. o.p. (4–6). These studies of desert wildlife picture with clarity and beauty the atmosphere of the desert (Student/Teacher Source).

REED, W. M., *Sky is Blue*, New York: Harcourt, Brace & World, Inc., 1940. (4–6). This elementary scientific book on geology and weather has a chapter (pp. 109–120) on "Why do we have deserts?" For good readers (Student/Teacher Source).

VII. *Generalizations to be Discovered. Citations of Proof*

A. Man adapts himself to his environment, both biologically and culturally, and adapts his environment to meet his own needs.

1. Nomadic people have adapted themselves to desert conditions.

2. The people of Israel have changed much of their desert environment to meet their own needs.

3. The early American colonists in both Jamestown and Massachusetts were forced to adapt themselves to their environment.

B. The harsher the physical environment the more time man must spend meeting his *basic needs* and the less time he has for *leisure*.

    1. Consider the early American frontiersman.

    2. Consider the Eskimo or the Aborigines of Australia.

C. *Natural* resources become valuable only when man uses them, and his manner of using them reflects the needs and level of *technology* in his *society*.

    1. Consider the value of oil deposits today as compared to the period before the British and American firms began to exploit them.

    2. Consider the contrasting technology used in coal mines today and in the past.

D. Since natural resources are limited and human wants relatively unlimited, every society has developed some means of allocating resources.

    1. Consider the market place in a capitalist country.

    2. Consider a quota or ration system.

E. All societies have some form of *law* and organization through which necessary activities are performed.

    1. Consider a modern urban government.

    2. Consider the social arrangement of an important Indian tribe, such as the Apache or Zuni.

F. Every *culture* attempts to perpetuate itself by transmitting its *values* and *mores* to the young.

G. Man's physical environment and climate interact to condition the daily activities of man.

    1. Consider the people of Asia during the monsoon season.

    2. Consider the mountainous people of the Himalayas or the people of a Maine coastal fishing village.

3. Contrast living in Florida with living in Alaska during the winter months.

H. The *population density* of an area is often in direct proportion to the suitability of the area in terms of the ways of making a living.

1. Consider the population density of the wheat farms of the Great Plains in terms of the ways of making a livelihood there.

2. Consider the population density of a major urban center in terms of the numerous ways of making a livelihood there.

I. The inter-relationship of man and his physical environment have contributed to diverse cultural development.

1. Consider the Indian tribes' cultures in terms of their respect and reverence for their physical environment.

2. Consider the Eskimo.

Andrew Jackson:
A Strong President

GRADE FOUR

I. Descriptive Statement

Only a few of the thirty-five men who have occupied the White House have been able to match the strength, forcefulness, and popularity that Andrew Jackson brought to the office of President of the United States. During his period in the White House, 1828-1836, and even during the presidency of his friend, Martin Van Buren, there were very few national issues or events which he failed to influence. Such was his strength of character, that the period is commonly referred to as the Age of Jackson.

II. Provocative or Leading Question

What evidence would you offer to support the view that Andrew Jackson made full use of the office of the president?

III. Suggested Disciplines (Interdisciplinary)

1. Political Science
2. History
3. Economics

IV. *Specific Skills to be Developed*

A. Students should prepare an outline map of the United States as it appeared in 1832. The states should be identified with the dates of their admission and their major economic resources. Territories and frontier lines should be marked off.

B. Introduce the students to the nature of biographical and autobiographical accounts and historical fiction. Ask the students to consider the strong and weak points of biography; autobiography, historical fiction. Ask the students to locate three different types of biographical accounts of Jackson; a synopsis; a commercial piece that might have appeared in a fashionable periodical; a detailed account in a good encyclopedia.

C. Have the students locate pictures of Andrew Jackson in various poses and actions, such as in *American Heritage* or *The Album of American History*, and prepare several paragraphs describing Jackson as his personality and career are outlined in the pictures. These paragraphs should include an appropriate title for the essay, a selected topical sentence, proper paragraph development, and the organizing of the essay content in a chronological order paralleling Jackson's life and career.

D. Many myths, legends, and half-truths have attached themselves to Andrew Jackson. Have each student choose and describe one of them and offer reasons why it might have come into being. Some of the students might be able to offer reasons why the myth or half-truth could not be entirely correct.

E. Ask students to develop the denotative and connotative aspects of the following concepts: presidential veto, patronage, tariff, sectionalism, cheap money, speculation, compromise, reform, and caucus.

V. *Answers to the Provocative or Leading Question*

A. Jackson instituted many new presidential practices and made extensive use of many old ones. During his eight years in office, he strengthened the office of president by:

1. using the veto power more than all the preceding presidents combined;

2. being the first president ever to use the pocket veto;

3. developing the spoils systems by which the president decided who would fill the many jobs offered by the Federal Government; (This form of patronage had both its merits and evils, however, for the president it meant increased power in the operation of the government.)

4. refusing to obey or enforce Supreme Court orders, when he felt they were not in the best interest of the people;

5. appealing to the people of South Carolina personally rather than through an agent, and by threatening the use of federal troops, with himself as field commander, if South Carolina tried to act on their threat to abrogate Federal law in the state;

6. attacking all forms of privilege and monopoly which he felt took advantage of the common man. The most celebrated attack on a monopoly was Jackson's war with Nicholas Biddle, the head of the Second Bank of the United States. When Jackson vetoed the Recharter Bill in 1832, Biddle retaliated by withdrawing bank credit and making loans tighter, expecting that the economic consequence would be blamed on Jackson's veto of the Recharter Bill. However, Jackson was too effective as a slogan maker, "Go see Nicholas Biddle" and too influential with the people to be defeated. Biddle, however, was not and the Jackson forces not only prevented the rechartering of the bank, but, right or wrong, actually caused the demise of the bank prior to 1836, its official terminal date.

B. Jackson, like most powerful men, did not only do things himself but provided the leadership and atmosphere where other reform movements could flourish. During his tenure in the White House, a great reform movement developed on behalf of the common man. Some elements of this reform movement include:

1. a strengthening of political democracy at the state level by making more political offices elective rather than appointed, by reducing property and religious qualification for

voting and holding office, and by reducing the terms of public officials, thereby increasing the people's control over their actions;

2. a strengthening of democrary in the election of the president by substituting national nominating conventions for a caucus, and by removing from state legislatures the right to nominate members to the electoral college and giving this right to the people (political parties);

3. a strengthening of the economic and political rights of the common man, who was encouraged to join and organize trade unions to ensure his rights; (Workers were permitted to organize unions, participate in strikes, and become political voters and officials.)

4. the fostering of several major social reform movements. Reform movements were formed to ensure the rights of women; to protect religious freedom; to abolish slavery; to offer free public education; to provide better care to the insane; to prohibit the consumption of liquor, and to offer better care and legal protection to criminals and debtors.

VI. Content Sources

A. Books and Periodicals

ANDRIST, RALPH K. and SCHLESINGER, ARTHUR M., *Andrew Jackson, Soldier, Statesman*, Wisconsin: E. M. Hale and Company (Student Source).

FAULKNER, H. U., *American Political and Social History*, 6th Ed. New York: Appleton-Century-Crofton, 1952 (Teacher Source).

FISH, C. R., *Rise of the Common Man*. New York: The Macmillan Company, 1927. (History of American Life vol. 16) (Teacher Source).

FOSTER, G. S., *Andrew Jackson*. New York: Charles Scribner's Sons, 1951 (Student Source).

MACY, JESSE, *Anti-Slavery Crusade*; a chronicle of the gathering storm. New Haven: Yale University Press, 1921. (Chronicles of America vol. 28) (Teacher Source).

Meadowcroft, E. L., *Story of Andrew Jackson*, Wisconsin: E. M. Hale and Company. (Student Source).

Schlesinger, A. M., Jr. (1917-) *Age of Jackson*. Little. 1945. abr. New Amer. Lib. pa. (Teacher Source).

Steele, William O., *Andy Jackson's Water Well*, E. M. Hale and Company. (Student Source).

VII. *Generalizations to be Discovered. Citations of Proof*

A. The existence of *humanitarian groups* in society is evidence of unsolved problems in that society and man's concern for those hurt by such problems.

1. Consider Lucretia Mott or Dorothea Dix.

2. Consider the present Civil Rights movement in the United States.

B. *Sectionalism* and *nationalism* are opposed to each other, the stronger one of them is, the weaker the other.

C. Where the number and kinds of legal procedures available to ensure fair treatment is limited or decreasing, the more likely it is that people, even those who would normally be law abiding, will resort to illegal means of securing fairness.

D. As technology and population increase, and the problems of *governing* become more complex, the powers of the *central government* are usually expanded often displacing powers previously held by lower levels of government.

1. Consider the federal agencies in the local community.

2. Consider the sources of government power in agrarian and unindustralized nations which were studied in grade three.

E. The nature and type of government of a nation can often be determined by the locus of political power; however, it is always true that the farther the source of power is removed from the people, the less likely the nation is democratic.

F. In every generation, *reformers* have sought to effect change and mold *society* to their own pattern.

1. Consider the proponents of social legislation in one of the daily newspapers.

2. Consider one of the local reform groups in the community.

G. In organizing governments, it is essential to endow the *rulers* with sufficient power and make provisions for holding them responsible for its proper use.

    1. Consider the powers of a local town official. What provisions have been made to safeguard against the official abusing the powers of his office?

    2. Consider the commander of the local Boy Scout or Girl Scout unit.

H. The changing needs of society are reflected in the modifications of old *institutions*, the development of new ones, and the disappearance of those institutions which are no longer responsive to the demands of society.

I. Practices, procedures, and beliefs about government and other social institutions remain in effect long after the reasons for their having come into being have disappeared.

Latin America and the U.S. 1898-1947: A Period of Changing Relations

GRADE FIVE

I. Descriptive Statement

The relationship of the United States and the countries of South America has rarely been the same for long periods of time. There have been periods of intense hatred and other periods of strong cooperation and solidarity between the two. Probably, at no time was their dislike and hatred for us stronger than in the period during and following the Spanish-American War. However, the termination of this period of mutual distrust and bitterness in the middle 1920's paved the way for more than two decades of unusually strong friendship during a most difficult and uncertain period of international relations.

II. Provocative or Leading Questions

What reasons might you cite for the intense hatred of the United States by Latin America in the period following the Spanish-American War and before the Good Neighbor Policy? What reasons could you offer to explain the reasons for the change of attitude from one of distrust and bitterness to one of friendship and cooperation, beginning in the late 1920's?

III. Suggested Disciplines (Interdisciplinary)

1. Political Science.   2. History.
3. Sociology.   4. Geography.

IV. Skills

A. Students should prepare a scale map of South America, Central America, and the Carribean Islands. Major topographic features will be identified by symbols of the geographer. Appropriate geographic map symbols should also indicate the major cities, and major industrial and agricultural products.

B. Students will be asked to decide on and prepare the features of a sociological study of the Latin American people today. The features of this study should require student groups to gather and organize the following data:

1. Prepare a demographic study of the people; this study would explore such items as population numbers, trends, dispersal, density, ratio of male to female, and so on.

2. Prepare a "social view" of the Latin American people; this would include data on the different religions and number of members, nationalities with number of members and major centers of residence, educational levels—number of college, high school, and grade level graduates, and illiterates.

3. Prepare an "economic view" of the Latin American people. This would include data on the occupational types and numbers, gross national product by country with rate of growth, per capita income, distribution of income, distribution of land ownership, land usage patterns, and so forth.

C. Students should be asked to identify the connotative aspects of the following social studies concepts: most favored nation clause, balance of payments, sovereignty, executive agreement, protectorate, political "recognition", imperialism, reciprocal trade agreement, and Pan-Americanism.

V. *Answers to the Provocative or Leading Questions*

A. The major reasons for the Latin American dislike and distrust of the "colossus of the north" following the Spanish-American War and until the late 1920's were:

1. The Spanish-American War itself left many Latin Americans opposed to the United States because the United States had fought and beaten their mother country of Spain, taken territory in the Caribbean, and had established a protectorate over the island of Cuba by forcing them to include the Platt Amendment in their constitution.

2. The Olney Interpretation of the Monroe Doctrine which presumed the sovereignty of the United States in the western hemisphere.

3. The philosophy of the Roosevelt Corollary which stated outright that the United States had the right to intervene in the affairs of Latin American countries under certain circumstances. This philosophy was enacted in Santo Domingo, Haiti, and Nicaragua resulting in U. S. troops being stationed in various Latin American countries, often for several years at a time.

4. The role of the United States in the Panama Revolution led to a bitter relationship between the Latin American nations, especially Colombia and the United States.

5. The policies of "dollar diplomacy" which were practiced in varying degrees by Theodore Roosevelt, William Howard Taft, and Woodrow Wilson, and especially by Harding and Coolidge, made United States commercial firms the possesors of many of the major industries of Latin America.

6. Woodrow Wilson's policy of Watchful Waiting toward the Mexican revolution and his subsequent dispatching of Pershing and an expeditionary force into Mexico helped to bring about several years of declining relations between the two nations.

B. The major reasons for the change in Latin America's attitude toward the United States from one of bitterness to one of friendliness and cooperation were:

1. The Dwight Morrow mission to Mexico led to the settlement of the dispute over compensation to American owners of Mexican mineral resources whose deeds had been revoked and property expropriated by the Mexican Government.

2. Hoover's withdrawal of American troops from Nicaragua, followed by Roosevelt's policy of removing all American troops from Latin American territory.

3. The Good Neoghbor Policy of Franklin D. Roosevelt which included:

(a) Promoting the idea of cooperation and friendship by fostering the Pan-American movement.

(b) Abrogating the Platt Amendment and thereby relinquishing all claims to Cuba, except the naval base at Guantanamo.

(c) Abrogating the policies which had characterized the Big Stick era.

(d) Establishing an import-export bank which loaned money to Latin America to purchase United States goods and increase trade.

(e) Making reciprocal trade agreements with many Latin American countries which partially eliminated the tariff barriers to trade between the United States and Latin America.

(f) Cancelling the traditional unilateral interpretation and enforcement of the Monroe Doctrine and replacing it with a multilateral approach which made the United States and Latin America equal partners in preserving the Monroe Doctrine.

C. Prior to and during World War II, the Pan-Americanism of the 1930's paid dividends in the form of cooperation of the United States and the Latin American nations, except Argentina, against the aggression of Germany and Italy. The United States and Latin America cooperated in all the following ways:

1. At the Buenos Aires Conference in 1936 they signed a pact pledging to consult with each other in the event of a threatened war.

2. At the Panama Conference of 1939 they jointly established a "safety zone" around their territories into which the war was not to be carried.

3. At the Havana Conference of 1940 they agreed not to let Germany have possession of the Dutch and French Latin American territories, even though Hitler's armies had taken the Mother Countries.

4. At Rio de Janeiro in 1942, the United States and Latin America met to plan a common course of action against the aggressors, and later in 1945 at Chapultepec, Mexico they pledged to defend each other's territory against aggression, both from within and without the Western Hemisphere.

5. At Rio in 1947 the Act of Chapultepec was fully implemented in the form of the Rio treaty which provided that an armed attack against any American state shall be considered an attack on all American states, and all signatories shall go to the aid of the attacked state.

VI. *Content Sources*

A. Books and Periodicals

BARR, GLENN, *Our Friends in South America*, New York: The Macmillan Company, 1950. (Student Source)

CARPENTER, FRANCES, *Our South American Neighbors*, New York: American Book Company, 1955. (Student Source)

CONSIDINE, R. B., *Panama Canal*, New York: Random House, 1951. (Teacher Source)

EPSTEIN, SAMUEL, and WILLIAMS, B. W., *First Book of Mexico*, New York: Franklin Watts, Inc. 1955. (Teacher/Student Source)

HENRY, MARGUERITE, *Chile, in Story and Pictures*, Racine, Wisc.: Whitman Publishing Co., 1941 (Teacher/Student Source)

PENDLE, GEORGE, *Argentina*, New York: The Macmillan Company, 1957. (Teacher Source)

QUINN, VERNON, *Picture Map Geography of South America*,

Philadelphia: J. B. Lippincott Co., 1941. (Teacher/Student Source)

Tor, Regina, *Getting to Know Puerto Rico*, New York, Coward-McCann, Inc., 1955. (Teacher/Student Source)

VII. Generalizations to be Discovered. Citations of Proof

A. The particular and peculiar movements of the earth in space result in varied conditions on its regional surfaces, and these conditions in turn, influence the daily activities of man.

1. Consider the change of season or the contrasting weather in Florida and Maine in the month of January.

2. Contrast a South American tropical rain forest with the desert lands of the Middle East.

B. *Feelings, ideas, and patterns of behavior* continue in existence long after the causes for their development have disappeared.

C. A nation's *sovereignty* is limited to the degree that its people, land, or government are under the control of another nation.

1. Consider the protectorate status of Cuba following the Spanish-American War.

2. Consider the status of Morocco in the early 1900's when Germany and France exercised considerable control there.

D. In the contemporary world, historical events have a significance beyond the time and place of their origin.

E. As *regional specialization* takes place, there is greater *interdependence* among trading regions and less *national self-sufficiency*.

1. Consider the organization and purposes of the Common Market.

2. Consider the trade relations among the British Commonwealth nations.

F. It is unique among modern man that he formulates *ideologies* to justify conduct.

1. Consider the reasons given as to why the U. S. Government felt it necessary to develop the atomic bomb.

2. Consider any public official's statements following an argumentative or questionable decision.

G. Both problems and achievements of the present have their roots in mankind's past.

1. Consider the attitude of Cuba toward the U. S. today and the reasons Cuba gives for this attitude.

2. Consider the long historical and often fruitless struggle to establish an institution such as the present United Nations.

H. One of the most difficult tasks of the historian is to analyze and interpret human motives and actions in terms of their being "good or bad" for mankind.

1. Consider Theodore Roosevelt's motives and actions in the Panamanian Revolution and the negotiating and building of the Panama Canal.

2. Consider the concept of "the white man's burden."

Issues of Sectionalism Following the Era of Good Feeling

GRADE EIGHT

I. Descriptive Statement

In the decade or so following the Treaty of Ghent, a great nationalism developed among the states which expressed itself both in foreign and domestic policies. However, this nationalism was short-lived, and by the election of 1824 the sections of the country had aligned themselves to the major issues of the period in a manner which was designed to safeguard and perpetuate their own self-interests, whether it be political, economic, or social. The resulting sectionalism was to wax and wane for more than 35 years until finally it was to burst into flames in 1861 at Fort Sumter, South Carolina.

II. Provocative or Leading Question

What were the major domestic issues which divided the sections of the country one against the other in the years following the Era of Good Feeling?

III. Suggested Disciplines (Interdisciplinary)

1. Political Science   3. Sociology
2. Economics   4. Geography

IV. Specific Skills to be Developed

A. Have the students trace the major episodes in the development of the states' rights theory, offering a cause and effect relationship to explain the major revisions of the theory in its course of development. This might then be summarized in the form of a time line.

B. During the discussions and assignments concerning Jackson's views on the Second Bank of the United States, the students should be asked to develop skills relating to money and its changing value under given economic conditions. The student might be asked to:

1. Prepare a simplified weighted index for the purchasing power of the dollar in selected years.

2. Prepare a supply and demand schedule for an important product of the period; cotton would be an excellent choice.

3. Have selected students explain such theories of money as the following:

(a) Gresham's Law,

(b) Quantity theory of money,

(c) Circulation of money theories.

C. Have students prepare a broken line graph indicating the effects of the various tariffs of the period on the balance of trade and balance of payments.

D. Have students develop the connotative aspects of several of the following concepts; balance of trade, protective tariff, slavery, Gresham's Law, cheap money, states' rights, Federalism, nullification, speculation, and compromise.

V. Answers to the Provocative or Leading Question

The major issues which divided the sections of the country and their respective viewpoints on these issues were:

A. The nature of the union

1. The north felt the Federal Constitution had created an indivisible Federal union from which no state or states could withdraw, and that matters involving several states (banking, commerce, immigration, and so forth) were decidedly under the scope of Federal, rather than state jurisdiction.

2. The South felt the union was a voluntary confederation of states, from which an individual state could legally withdraw, and that the powers of government which had not been specifically delegated to Congress in Article I, Section 8, Clauses 1–17 of the U. S. Constitution had been reserved to the states. For the most part, the southern states subscribed to a theory of states' rights, including nullification and right of secession, which would severely limit the powers of the Federal Government.

3. The western states agreed with the view of the northern states, though the border states had major factions supporting each viewpoint.

B. On the tariff issue

1. The North favored the tariff because it was legal, produced revenue, stimulated the export industry, and protected import industries.

2. The South opposed the tariff because it had few industries to be protected; the tariff raised the prices of commodities and it caused other nations to raise the tariff rates against southern cotton, rice, and other major exports.

3. The West was divided on the tariff question. A very strong faction opposed the tariff on primarily the same grounds used by the southern states; however, there was a significant faction that favored the tariff when the revenue was used for the building of internal improvements.

C. On the immigration issue

1. The North favored an unrestricted immigration policy because: The immigrants provided a cheap source of labor, a consuming market, and brought about increased representation in the House of Representatives. Other more humanitarian motives were undoubtedly part of the reasons for the North's partiality to unrestricted immigration.

2. The South eventually developed a strong opposition to unrestricted immigration because: the immigrant did not come south; the North gained strength in Congress; many organized groups opposed certain nationalities for a variety of reasons, some being outright prejudice. There were, how-

ever, many southern people who did not share the majority opinion on the issue of immigration.

3. The West favored unrestricted immigration because: the immigrant provided a market for farm goods; many immigrants came west and helped territories to qualify for statehood, and the westward movement of immigrants and others brought pressure on the Federal government to expand internal improvements, military protection, and other services to the western territories.

D. On the national bank issue

1. The North favored the national bank because: It was a source of hard money; extended credit to businessmen; controlled irregular state banking practices, and was a good investment for businessmen.

2. The South opposed the national bank because: They felt it was unconstitutional; it served the interests of the industrial North but not the agrarian South; it had become a political tool; it followed a hard money policy; and the money supply in the South did not meet their needs.

3. The West generally opposed the national bank for many of the same reasons as expressed by the South. It also opposed the bank because the hard money policy often made it difficult to purchase western land, except from speculators.

E. On the extension of slavery

1. The North opposed any extension of slavery because: Many felt the institution of slavery was illegal and unholy; the extension of slavery would permit the South to increase its strength in the Congress and in the electoral college, and extending slavery would open up new territories which might be an attraction to factory workers and newly arrived immigrants.

2. The South favored the extension of slavery because: It perpetuated and expanded slavery and opened up new lands for cotton production; it increased the influence of the South in the Federal government and it occasionally brought the South and western territories, especially the border areas, and western states into stronger partnerships.

3. The West was generally opposed to the extension of slavery because: Most westerners opposed the institution of slavery itself; the slaves provided the labor which immigrants and settlers would have otherwise provided. Many Westerners favored the extension of slavery, particularly when the effect was to force the Federal government to open up new western lands or to lower the price of western land.

F. On the issue of internal improvements

1. The North was divided on this issue. Many felt that internal improvements would lead to increased trade with the West, however, others felt that internal improvements would mean new taxes and the loss of eastern factory workers. Some northerners favored internal improvements when the tariff revenue would be used for construction; this, in turn, encouraged the West to vote for and favor the tariff.

2. The South opposed internal improvements at Federal expense because: The water trade routes met most of the needs of the South; the South did not trade very much with the West, where the internal improvements would be constructed; internal improvement would increase the trade of the North and West and might reduce the North-South trade; the revenue for internal improvements occasionally came from tariff revenue.

3. The West greatly favored internal improvements because: Western settlers were encouraged to occupy the territories; they provided a means to get export goods to shipping centers at reduced costs.

VI. *Content Sources*

A. Books and Periodicals

ADAMS, J. T. et al. eds. *Album of American History,* 1783–1853. vol. 2 New York: Charles Scribner's Sons, 1945 Teacher/Student Source).

DAUGHERTY, S. V. *Ten Brave Women.* Philadelphia: J. B. Lippincott Co., 1953. Chapter on Dorothea Dix (Student Source).

FISH, C. R. *Rise of the Common Man.* New York: The

Macmillan Company, 1927. (History of American Life vol. 16) (Teacher Source).

FOSTER, G. S. *Andrew Jackson*. New York: Charles Scribner's Sons, 1951 (Student Source).

MACY, JESSE. *Anti-slavery crusade; a chronicle of the gathering storm*. New Haven: Yale University Press. 1921. (Chronicles of America vol 28) (Teacher Source).

SCHLESINGER, A. M., JR. (1917-) *Age of Jackson*. Little. 1945. abr. New Amer. Lib. pa. (Teacher Source).

STEVENS, W. O. *Famous American Statesmen*. New York: Dodd Mead & Co., 1953. Considers Clay, Webster, Calhoun, Madison, Monroe, Jackson (Student Source).

VII. *Generalizations to be Discovered. Citations of Proof*

A. People develop *political institutions* in the way they do in order to achieve what they consider to be the best form of society and the best way of life.

    1. Consider the Massachusetts theocratic government during the colonial period.

    2. Consider the evolution of the British political system in response to the changing concept of the best form of society and the best way of life.

B. Intense *loyalty* to a local political and cultural unit *(sectionalism)* inhibits loyalty to a greater political and cultural unit *(nationalism)*.

    1. Consider the difficulty of Chiang Kai Shek in bringing the Chinese provinces into a loyal relationship to the central government.

    2. Consider the difficulty of Germany or Italy in unifying the local political units into a national state.

C. Cultural isolation and *ethnocentrism* inhibit intercultural understanding.

    1. Consider the isolationist policies of the United States following World War I.

    2. Consider the isolation of China before the Opium War.

D. The *values* of a society are reflected in the *institutions* of that society and the *status* assigned to the various institutions.

1. Consider the great importance of engineers and scientists and their organizations in the Soviet Union.

2. Consider the Chinese institutions which reflect the Confucian philosophy.

E. The absence of *legal procedures* for changing governments will often encourage people to resort to illegal and covert means of changing the government.

F. The locus or source of *political power* will vary according to the type of government, however, in a *dictatorship*, its possessors will be few in number as opposed to a *democracy* where the possessors will be the people themselves.

1. Consider the source of power in the British Government today as compared with early British history.

2. Consider the real source of power in the Soviet Union, even though they have a very democratic constitution.

G. In every society, the installed *power structure* will be challenged by *reformers* who seek to bring about change and shape the society to their own design.

1. Consider the Abolitionists of the pre-Civil War period.

2. Consider the present Civil Rights movement.

3. Consider the Populists of the 1890's and early 1900's.

H. Though there are variations among individuals in terms of *race*, *religion*, and *nationality*, these variations do not necessarily imply inequality.

I. In a *democracy*, a *compromise* between the *rights* of the individual citizen and the common welfare is a constantly recurring problem which is best solved by the *judiciary*.

J. People express a preference for their own cultural and political system by using the *mores*, practices, and standards of their society to measure other peoples and other societies.

1. Consider the view of the "New Immigrants" by Americans following World War I.

2. Consider the view most civilized cultures have of the "uncivilized African" and his institutions.

China
and Imperialism

GRADE NINE

I. Descriptive Statement

A continuing problem of the Far East since the early years of the nineteenth century has been imperialism. Both of the two major Far Eastern nations, China and Japan, have been imperialistic; and China, in particular, was a victim of other imperialistic nations for more than a century. This unit focuses on the experiences of China with imperialism, but also indicates how China's experiences impinge on her Far Eastern neighbors.

II. Provocative or Leading Question

Beginning with the Opium War, how would you describe the experiences of China with imperialism?

III. Suggested Disciplines (Interdisciplinary)

1. Geography   2. Political Science (International Relations)
3. Economics   4. Sociology

IV. Specific Skills to be Developed

A. Prepare a detailed outline map of China on the eve of the Opium War. Mark-off the major physiographic features and boundaries of the provinces. Color in the spheres of influence established by the western powers, and indicate the occupying western power for each sphere of influence and the date when it became such.

B. Prepare a time line for China and for Japan showing the major events of each in their relationship with imperialism. The time line should cover the period from the Opium War to the present and should be organized in such a way as to indicate the respective periods when Japan and China were victims or perpetrators of imperialism.

C. Compare and contrast the *motives* of two imperialistic powers and the *methods* and *characteristics* of their imperialism in the subjugated territories. Excellent examples for contrast would be the British in India, and the Belgians in Africa. This attempt to compare and contrast imperialism should coincide with the students' grasping of the nature of imperialism as a developmental process.

D. Develop the denotative and connotative aspects of the following concepts: extra-territoriality, sovereignty, imperialism, satellite, sphere of influence, protectorate, white man's burden, aggression, and most favored nation clause.

V. *Answers to the Provocative or Leading Question*

The Experience of China with Imperialism

In the early nineteenth century, the imperialist powers of Europe were attracted to China as a place to market goods, a source of cheap labor, a country with valuable minerals and resources which the Chinese were neglecting, because Europe's people desired Chinese tea and silk; and because China was unable to defend herself against the military and industrial nations of Europe.

Following the Opium War of 1842, western imperialism took hold in China. Mineral resources were taken or bought; coolie labor was drafted or hired; local government and villages came under the sway of the imperialists; special privileges were granted the imperialists in trading relations, including monopolies over certain products; special laws and exemptions from certain Chinese laws were part of the imperialism, including the concept of extra-territoriality; and spheres of influence were carved out of China by the imperialist power. Of all the major world powers, only the United States did not actively participate in this subjugation of China. The other western powers had their own spheres of influence, concessions, and special privileges in China.

In addition to the western powers, Japan followed her victories in the Sino-Japanese War of 1894–95 by annexing Formosa and claiming Korea as a sphere of influence; Korea was officially annexed in 1910. Japan further extended her imperialism in China following the Russo-Japanese War of 1904–05. The Treaty of Portsmouth ending the war permitted Japan to take from Russia the Chinese territories of Port Arthur and a sphere of influence in southern Manchuria.

In 1899 the John Hay circular letters announced the United States' Open Door Policy toward China, requesting equal trading rights for all nations in China. Later, the Open Door Policy was expanded to include the preserving of China's integrity and independence. The 1900 Boxer Rebellion against the imperialist powers led to serious humiliation for the Chinese people as well as heavy indemnity charges. Had it not been for the support of the U. S., the imperialist powers might have divided China among themselves.

During World War I, the Japanese would have forced China to her knees and deprived her of what limited sovereignty she retained if they had been successful in forcing China to agree to the Twenty-One Demands. China, with the support of the U. S., was able to withstand the Japanese pressure and forced the withdrawal of many of the demands. During and following the war, the Japanese did seize and later return territories of China which had belonged to defeated Germany.

In the 1920's at the Washington Conference, treaties were signed by the major western powers agreeing to respect the independence and integrity of China. However, in 1931 Japan invaded and conquered Manchuria, and began to develop it into a major industrial base for further military advances. In 1937, Japan launched a full attack against China, initiating the Far Eastern phase of World War II. Japan soon conquered more than one-quarter of the country, but was unable to subjugate the defeated provinces or to occupy the rest of China. Some of the western powers, including the U. S., offered a limited amount of aid to China but did not actually send troops to ward off the Japanese advances. During the course of the struggles in both Asia and Europe, many of the western imperialist powers were forced to evacuate their spheres of influence and devote all their manpower and materials to defending their homelands.

Once the European phase of the war intensified and the Americans entered the war, considerable aid in the form of both men and supplies was sent to help the Chinese in their war with Japan. During the war, both the U. S. and England relinquished their general privileges, including extra-territoriality, in China and pledged that Manchuria and Formosa would be returned to China after the war. In 1945, when the end of the war still appeared far off, the Big Three met at Yalta and made several momentous decisions pertaining to China. The concluded agreements provided for the following:

1. The U.S.S.R. would enter the war against Japan within three months following the defeat of Germany and would conclude a pact of friendship and alliance with the Chinese Nationalist (as opposed to Communist) Government.

2. The U.S.S.R. was guaranteed by England and the U. S. that:

   (a) the status quo in Outer Mongolia would be preserved,

   (b) Russia would have Southern Sakhalin and adjacent islands,

   (c) Russia would have a lease on Port Arthur, preeminent interests in Darien, and would be given possession of the Kurile Islands, and

   (d) a joint Sino-Soviet stock company would manage the Chinese Eastern Railroad and the South-Manchurian Railroad, however, China would be assured of sovereignty over Manchuria.

Following the war and the removal of the Japanese, the internal struggle, which has been waxing and waning in China for more than twenty five years, engulfed the entire country. With tremendous support from the U.S.S.R. the Chinese Communists waged a bitter war and by 1949 had forced the Nationalists to escape to the offshore islands. A People's Republic of China under Mao Tse-Tung was proclaimed as the new government of China. It adopted communistic methods in its political and economic systems, while simultaneously removing all traces of western influences from Chinese society. Practically all western people, including missionaries, reporters, and humanitarian groups, were forced to leave the mainland. The western cultural and educational institutions were destroyed and replaced by communistic ones.

During the Chinese Civil War, 1945-49, the U.S.S.R. had provided military aid and advice to the Chinese Communists. The U.S.S.R. recognized the Chinese Communist Government within 24 hours after its creation, and in February, 1950 concluded a major agreement with Mao Tse-Tung which constituted an alliance of the two nations in many matters of politics, economics, and international affairs. In addition, the treaty provided that China would recognize the status of Outer Mongolia, and that Soviet Russia could continue to occupy Port Arthur until 1952, when it would revert to the Chinese Communists.

Since the establishment of the People's Republic of China, the country has gradually chartered an imperialistic course against its neighboring countries. These imperialistic attempts have included:

    1. In 1951 Red China seized the country of Tibet and claimed it as Chinese territory. Eight years later when the Tibetans revolted, the revolt was brutally suppressed and the Dalai Lama and others were forced to seek refuge in India. Subsequent events led to bitter hostilities between India and Communist China, portending future border clashes.

    2. In 1958, the Chinese Communists bombarded the offshore islands of Quemoy and Matsu and claimed the islands. With the aid of the U. S., the Nationalist Chinese were able to prevent any attempt of the Communists to actually occupy the islands.

    3. In 1950, the Chinese Communists urged and supported the attack of the North Koreans against the South Koreans,

and later entered the war herself. This conflict lasted until 1953 when a truce was concluded; however, North Korea is still under the control of the Chinese Communists and remains a danger to South Korea and the stability of the Far East.

4. Between 1946-54, Red China aided Ho Chi Minh and the communists and sympathizers of Vietnam to fight and win the struggle against the French. The 1954 Geneva Convention divided Vietnam at the 17th parallel, with North Vietnam under communist control. Subsequently, the North Vietnamese, with the support and aid of Red China, aided the Viet Cong in its attempt to overthrow the South Vietnam government. Similar efforts were made to aid the Pathet Lao to capture the Laotian Government and establish a Chinese Communist puppet state.

5. Red China has demanded from the other major Communist power, the U.S.S.R., that territories claimed by the U.S.S.R. in Central Asia bordering on Sinkiang Province, the Amur River valley, and Vladivostok, be returned to Communist China.

6. The specific roles played by Red China in Africa, Cuba, Cambodia, and Albania are not clear; however, in each of these areas there is undeniable evidence that Red China has been influential in their political development, though it is thought that she has not been able to establsh an imperialistic relationship with any of them as of yet.

VI. Content Sources

A. Books and Periodicals

FAIRBANKS, J. K. and REESCHAUER, E. O., *East Asia, The Great Tradition*, Boston: Houghton-Mifflen Company, 1960 (Teacher Source).

BARNETT, A. DOAK, *Communist China and Asia: Challenge to American Policy*, Council on Foreign Relations, New York: Harper & Row, Publishers, 1960 (Teacher Source).

CHIANG KAI-SHEK, *Soviet Russia in China*, New York. Farrar, Straus & Giroux, Inc., 1957 Teacher Source).

ROSINGER, LAWRENCE K., *China's Wartime Politics*, 1937–44, Princeton, N. J.: 1944 (Teacher Source).

CAMERSON, M. E. et al. *China, Japan and the Powers*, New York: The Ronald Press Company, 1952 (Student Source).

DURDIN, and SMITH, R.A., *China and the World*, Foreign Policy Association, 1953 (Student Source).

PRUDEN, DURWARD and STEINBERG, SAMUEL. *Colonialism Yesterday, Today, and Tomorrow*, New York: Oxford Book Co., Inc., 1957 (Student Source).

VII. *Generalizations to be Discovered. Citations of Proof*

A. To the degree that a nation is under the influence of *imperialist powers*, its own *sovereignity* is limited.

1. Consider the protectorate status of Cuba under the Platt Amendment.

2. Consider Morocco under the control of the French prior to World War I.

B. Internally warring factions will cease or at least diminish their own struggle and join the common cause when both perceive an external threat as mutually threatening.

1. Consider the U. S. home front following the bombing of Pearl Harbor.

2. Consider China following the Japanese invasion in 1937.

C. *Treaties, agreements,* and pacts among peoples are no more valuable than the respect shown for their provisions, regardless of the validity and legality of the documents themselves.

1. Consider treaties among the Indians and U. S. government.

2. Consider the Ribbentrop-Molotov Nonaggression Treaty.

D. In the contemporary world, peoples have developed rather rational and systematic *philosophies* to explain and justify conduct.

1. Consider the policy statements of the U. S. and Red China in their relations to each other.

2. Consider the explanations offered by India and Pakistan as a result of the continued dispute over Kashmir.

E. All peoples tend to judge others in terms of their own cultural standards and mores, thereby expresssing partiality for their own culture.

1. Consider the African's view of the Belgian imperialists.

2. Consider the supercilious attitude of the Chinese toward the early western imperialists.

F. *Cultural isolation* and *ethnocentrism* inhibit intercultural understanding.

1. Consider the U. S. policies of isolation in its early history.

2. Consider the Hermit Kingdom of Korea prior to Chinese possession.

G. The prime mover for imperialism has traditionally been economic, however, *imperialism* itself touches all aspects of society.

1. Consider the interest of the U. S. in the Philippines.

2. Consider the interest of England in Egypt.

H. As *technology* and *communication* bring all parts of the world close, the national and international policies of one nation has impact on more and more nations.

The Communists Impose a Dictatorship on the Russian People

GRADE TEN

I. Descriptive Statement

The establishment of a Communist government in Czarist Russia during World War I was a historical event of rarely paralelled importance and one that few people ever thought possible. This Communist dictatorship, like all dictatorships, was not long in taking the shape which makes dictatorships so easily recognized.

II. Provocative or Leading Questions

What conditions in Czarist Russia did the Communists capitalize on to establish their dictatorship? What steps were taken to solidify their position in the decade following the revolution?

III. Suggested Disciplines (Interdisciplinary)

1. History   2. Political Science   3. Economics
4. Geography   5. Sociology

IV. *Specific Skills to be Developed*

A. Analyze and summarize the Marxist arguments that the worker is exploited by the capitalist; include clear definitions of terms such as: labor, value, surplus value, exploitation, capitalist, profit, and class struggle. Prepare a chart indicating the basic tenets of Marxism, and then parallel these tenets with the present practices of the Soviet Union, being sure to indicate where the tenets and practices agree or disagree.

B. Draw an outline map of the U.S.S.R. as it is today. Within this outline, indicate the previous geographic boundaries of territory under the Czars. Identify the major physiographic elements of the U.S.S.R., including their climatic and vegetational zones.

C. Bar graphs should be prepared on two contrasting areas of the U.S.S.R., such as the Crimea and one of the most eastern republics, showing the great variability among the areas of the U.S.S.R. in terms of:

    1. population density and urbanization,

    2. major agricultural crops or industrial products,

    3. nationalities and religions of the inhabitants,

    4. climatic zones.

D. Prepare an organizational chart of the government of the Soviet Union and a similar chart for the Communist Party of the Soviet Union. Show the interrelationship among several positions in the two organizations by means of broken lines or dots.

E. Prepare graphs on any of the following:

    1. the agricultural production of the Soviet Union in selected years, and several important individual agricultural commodities such as cotton, meat, and grains;

    2. the industrial production of the Soviet Union in selected years, including specific industrial products such as heavy machinery, electricity, and home appliances;

    3. the population of the Soviet Union. This graph would indicate: total population in selected years, ratio of male to female, age distribution, major occupational divisions, and percentage of people who are urbanized or agrarian.

V. *Answers to the Provocative or Leading Questions*

A. The conditions in Czarist Russia on the eve of the Revolution were most conducive to the aims of any revolutionary group. They included the following:

1. Many of the people were bitter against the leaders of the government, and often the Czar himself, for the Revolution of 1905 and the bloody manner of suppressing the outbreaks. Though the Revolution of 1905 was followed by several liberal measures, including the establishment of a legislature called a Duma to pass laws for the country, many of these measures were only ineffectually acted on, and the Duma itself soon became a debating society.

2. There were many groups in Czarist Russia who wanted an end to Czarist government, and its tactics of repression and denial of liberty.

3. The end of the nineteenth Century had brought about the beginnings of an industrial revolution in Russia. This industrial revolution was the impetus for great numbers of peasants to move into the cities and take toiling jobs in the factories and mines. These workers were highly discontented because of poor living conditions, high taxes, and the denial of an effective voice in government.

4. Though the serfs of Russia had been freed in 1861, the government had permitted so many conditions and attachments to be imposed on them by their previous owners, the nobility, that in many cases the freed peasant was actually in a worse position than he had been as a serf. In particular, the peasant was in continuous debt, without land of his own, living in the most wretched of conditions, and not at all sure of having the essentials of life.

5. The Industrial Revolution had created a commercial middle class who demanded an effective voice in the government.

6. Many nationalities in Russia felt the Czarist government followed a policy of Russification which discriminated against them. Several desired to secede from Czarist Russia and establish countries and governments of their own.

B. The entrance of Czarist Russia into World War I aggravated already crucial problems and brought other new critical problems into being. Problems caused by entrance into the war include:

1. The civilian populace and many soldiers were disaffected when it was discovered that the Russian soldiers were fighting with ineffective equipment and supplies, and the nobility was providing poor military leadership. These conditions of poor fighting equipment and leadership caused high casualties and one military defeat after another, which led to chaos both on the battle front and the home front.

2. Chaos reigned among the civilian populace due to the demands of the military units for priority on all matters of food, medical supplies, transportation, and war materials. The home front was not able to withstand these pressures, and consequently the cities were without transportation, food was rationed or simply unavailable, and what was already a difficult life became intolerable.

3. The pressures of the war brought many adherents to the revolutionary theories of the Bolsheviks, particularly when the Bolsheviks demanded the three items the people most desired: land would be taken from the estates and distributed among the peasants; Russia would withdraw from the war; and the Russian people would be provided food (bread) once the peasants were able to farm their own land and the pressures of the war ended.

C. The conditions in Czarist Russia in 1917, in addition to the Bolshevik organization, leadership, and opportunism were sufficient to topple the Kerensky Government.

During the next twenty or so years, a major part of the efforts of the Bolsheviks was to solidify their hold on the government and to begin to institute programs of Communism. Immediately following the revolution, the Russian Communists tried to gain the support of the people in the internal war against the Whites. To gain the support of the people, Lenin and Trotsky took the following steps:

1. Russia agreed to accept the stringent peace terms of the

Treaty of Brest-Litovsk and thereby withdrew from World War I.

2. They ordered the peasants to seize the estates of the nobility and to claim the property in the name of the new Communist government. This land was soon nationalized, thereby preventing individual ownership by the peasants.

3. They ordered the factory workers to seize the plants and industries in the name of the Communist government. These, too, were nationalized by the government.

D. Following the Bolshevik Revolution, the next four years were occupied with preserving the revolution against the Whites and the foreign nations which aided the Whites. The Communists were successful in their efforts to crush the Whites due primarily to:

1. the lack of complete support by the Allies for the Whites; (The allies, having been involved in war for more than three years, did not look forward to becoming involved in any internal struggle. On the other hand, the threat of foreign intervention aroused the Russian people in support of the Reds.)

2. the ability of Trotsky to organize an effective Red Army, while the leaders of the White forces were dispersed and arguing among themselves;

3. the support of the new Communist government by the peasant and factory workers, who were determined to prevent the capitalists and nobility from regaining the estates and factories which had been expropriated.

E. By 1921, the rule of Communists over Russia was no longer questionable, and political recognition by other nations, including the U.S. in 1933, was soon forthcoming. During the next seven years, following the failure of War Communism, the Communists were reluctant to force their programs on the people until the ravages of war had been reduced. Between 1921 and 1928, the new government adopted the New Economic Policy (NEP) which permitted a limited form of capitalism to flourish in Communist Russia. This economic policy was designed to give the Marxist planners sufficient time to formulate a Marxist economic program while at the same time not impeding recovery from World War I and the internal struggle. In political matters, however, the new Communist leaders took immediate steps to solidify their power.

1. All political parties, other than the Communist Party, were prohibited.

2. A secret police was formed to subdue or eliminate political opponents.

3. The government of the country and the Communist Party became virtually one and the same thing.

4. Political freedom, in the real sense of the term, disappeared. Newspapers, community organizations of all types and purposes, schools and colleges, and all elements of society publicized and followed the party line.

F. Following the death of Lenin in 1924, a bitter and lengthy struggle for leadership was waged between Stalin and Trotsky. Stalin's victory in this struggle by 1929 marked the coup de grace for the New Economic Policy and the return to a total policy of Communism in all areas of life. Once Stalin had assumed dictatorial power in both the government and the party, the Communists implemented programs more consonant with their own interpretation of Marxism. These programs included:

1. The beginning of central collective planning and the implementation of a series of Five Year Plans which were designed to industrialize Soviet Russia. This industrialization would be financed by imposing hardships on the peasant and farmer.

2. The "war on Kulaks" meant the end of a middle class group of peasants, and the beginning of herding the peasants into collective farms, thereby depriving them of the rights of private ownership of property.

3. The elimination of all opposition in all areas of society to the new Communist programs. Labor unions, education, communications media, religious groups and all other social institutions were placed under the control of the government and party.

G. By the late 1920's, there could be little mistaking the

characteristics of the country as those which earmarked it as communistic and governed by dictatorship .

VI. Content Sources

A. Books and Periodicals

BOWLES, CHESTER, *New Dimensions of Peace*. New York: Harper & Row Publishers, 1955. Analysis of revolutions in Russia, China, India (Teacher Source).

CRONYN, G. W., *A Primer on Communism; 200 questions and answers*. New York: E. P. Dutton & Co., Inc., 1960 (Student Source).

HARRIS, C. D., "U.S.S.R. Resources: I—Heavy Industry," *Focus*, vol. 5, No. 6, February 1955 (Teacher Source).

HARRIS, C. D., "U.S.S.R. Resources: II—Agriculture," *Focus*, vol. 5, No. 9. May 1955 (Teacher Source).

KETCHUM, R. M., ed., *What is Communism?* New York: E. P. Dutton & Co., Inc., 1955 (Student Source).

LENGYEL, EMIL, *The Soviet Union—the Land and its People*. New York: Oxford Book Co., Inc., 1951. (Oxford social studies pamphlets) (Student Source).

NATIONAL INDUSTRIAL CONFERENCE BOARD, Inc., *Statistical Handbook of the U.S.S.R.* The Board. 1957. pa. (Studies in Business Economics No. 55) (Teacher Source).

VII. Generalizations to be Discovered. Citations of Proof

A. As the powers of government are concentrated in the hands of a few, the possibility of *dictatorship* increases and the possibility of *democracy* decreases.

1. Consider Nazi Germany following 1933.

2. Consider the concepts of separation of powers and division of powers as they operate in the U.S. Government.

B. *Governments*, to be effective, must be responsive to changing needs and demands, which, in turn, are reflected by evolving *social institutions*.

1. Consider the Articles of Confederation and its failure to meet the needs of the people following the Revolution.

2. Consider the response in the American Colonies to the colonial governments when they were slow to recognize William and Mary as the new leaders of England.

C. Government officials must be given sufficient *authority* to carry out their responsibilities; however they must be held responsible for the manner in which they use their powers.

D. The source of *political power* will vary according to the form of government, however, in a *democracy* it will always emanate from the people.

1. Consider the Declaration of Independence.

2. Consider the source of political power in Nazi Germany, Fascist Italy, or Communist China.

E. Since the tasks of society can only be done in an organized manner, it is impossible to prevent the ordering and *stratification* of the people who are responsible for carrying out tasks.

1. Consider the class stratification of any industrialized society.

2. Consider class stratification even among Indian tribes.

F. Man develops his fullest potential in a society where *freedom* is permitted and *incentives* are available to reward individual efforts.

G. Each society rewards its workers in accordance with the *value* it assigns to that worker's contribution to society; however, the *value* is not static but a function of the *supply and demand* for each category of worker.

1. Consider the pay of unskilled labor in practically all societies.

2. Consider the changing value assigned to public educators in the United States.

H. Every *culture* attempts to maintain itself by transmitting its *values* and *mores* to the young.

I. No society displays an even development of *civilization* and human progress.

1. Consider the great advances made by the Japanese in technology and their contrasting treatment of the war victims.

2. Consider the great industrial advances made by the U.S.S.R. and their contrasting restrictions on individual freedom.

J. Every society has an *economic system* of some kind which attempts to bring together individual effort in the production of *goods and services.*

1. Consider the Italian Corporate State.

2. Consider the market system of the United States.

K. Though societies use both formal and informal devices of *social control,* the more industrialized and complex the society, the greater reliance the society puts on *formal controls* (laws, governments, social agencies, and so forth).

L. The *educational system* of a society reflects the values and priorities of that society.

1. Consider the educational system of colonial America.

2. Consider the old education system of China when its great emphasis was to produce civil servants.

M. As a nation industrializes, *occupational specialization* increases and this, in turn, influences the *class structure* and *stratification* in society.

Concepts—Generalizations —Structures

ANDERSON, HOWARD R. et al, *High School Social Studies Perspectives*, New York: Houghton Mifflin Co.

BERELSON, BERNARD, and STEINER, GARY A. *Human Behavior, An Inventory of Scientific Findings.* New York: Harcourt, Brace & World, Inc., 1964. (Excellent source of generalizations, supported by research.)

BLOOM, BENJAMIN S. (editor). *Taxonomy of Educational Objectives: Handbook I, Cognitive Domain.* New York: McKay, 1956. (Presents a classification system for educational objectives; helpful to all curriculum workers.)

Council for Advancement of Secondary Education, 1201 16th St. N.W., Washington, D. C. *Key Understandings in Economics*

ELAM, STANLEY. *Education and the Structure of Knowledge.* Chicago: Rand McNally & Co., 1964. (Eight men discuss "structure" generally and in specific subject disciplines.)

FORD, G. W. and PUGNO, LAWRENCE (editors). *The Structure of Knowledge and the Curriculum.* Chicago: Rand McNally & Co., 1964. (Discusses "structure" generally, then as related to different subject disciplines.)

GAGE, N. L. *Handbook of Research on Teaching.* Chicago: Rand McNally & Co., 1963. (An excellent reference that should help educators realize how little we "know" about teaching. For instance, a good theoretical section on concepts.)

HANNA, PAUL R. and LEE, JOHN R. "Generalizations from the Social Sciences," in *Social Studies in Elementary Schools*, John U. Michaelis (editor). Thirty-second Yearbook of the National Council for the Social Studies. Washington, D.C.: the Council 1962. pp. 62–89. (A description of a project at Stanford University, to select social science generalizations for use in the elementary school curriculum.)

HARRIS, CHESTER W. (editor). *Encyclopedia of Educational Research*. New York: Macmillan Co., 1960. (A basic reference; a starting point. See such topics as "Curriculum," and "Concepts.")

JONES, SAMUEL H., *Generalizing in the Social Science Classroom*, Social Education 21: p. 358–362, December 1957.

MASSIALAS, BYRON G. and KAZAMIAS, ANDREAS M., *Crucial Issues in the Teaching of Social Studies—A book of Readings*. New Jersey: Prentice-Hall, Inc., Englewood Cliffs.

NAGEL, ERNEST, *The Structure of Science: Problems in the Logic of Scientific Explanation*, New York: Harcourt, Brace & World, Inc., 1961, 618 pp.

National Council for the Social Studies in San Francisco, *Curriculum Planning in American Schools: The Social Studies*, A draft report prepared for consideration at the November 1958 meeting of the National Council for the Social Studies in San Francisco, by the Council's National Commission on the Social Studies.

PHENIX, PHILIP H., *Realms of Meaning*, New York: McGraw-Hill Book Co., Inc.

SAVETH, EDWARD N., *American History and the Social Sciences*, Free Press of Glencoe, Inc., 1964, 599 pp.

SHAVER, JAMES P., *Education Research and Instruction for Critical Thinking*, Social Education 25: p. 13–16, January 1962.

TURNER, GORDON B. et al, *The Social Studies and the Social Sciences*, Sponsored by the American Council of Learned Societies and the National Council for the Social Studies, New York: Harcourt, Brace & World, Inc.

WOMACK, JAMES G. (editor). *BOCES Social Studies Report*, Huntington, New York: Board of Cooperative Educational Services 1965.

Index

⋰⋱ ABOUT THE AUTHOR ⋰⋱

JAMES G. WOMACK received his undergraduate degree from Missouri University and a Master of Arts in Teaching from Harvard. He is an experienced public school teacher, having taught in Newton, Massachusetts and South Huntington, Long Island, New York and has served as the Assistant to the Director of the Henry George School of Economics in Boston. He is presently the Director of the Cooperative Review Service for Suffolk County, Long Island, New York and Assistant Director of the Cooperative Social Studies Project being sponsored by the Board of Cooperative Educational Services (BOCES) under the direction of Dr. Ernest Weinrich. Mr. Womack has written vocabulary manuals, prepared curriculum newsletters for local school systems, edited the *BOCES Social Studies Manuals* and served as consultant to the Bureau of Social Studies of the New York State Education Department, as well as several local school systems. He is currently conducting a series of inservice workshops under the auspices of BOCES to help train teachers in the new methodology for social studies.